Unless otherwise indicated, all Scripture quotations are taken from the King James Version (KJV) of the Bible.

Scripture quotations marked (NIV) are taken from the HOLY BIBLE, NEW INTERNATIONAL VERSION®. NIV®. Copyright© 1973, 1978, 1984 by International Bible Society. Used by permission of Zondervan. All rights reserved.

Scripture quoted by permission. Quotations designated (NET) are from the NET Bible® copyright ©1996-2006 by Biblical Studies Press, L.L.C. www.bible.org All rights reserved.

Scripture quotations marked (RSV) are taken from the Revised Standard Version of the Bible, copyright 1952 [2nd edition, 1971] by the Division of Christian Education of the National Council of the Churches of Christ in the United States of America. Used by permission. All rights reserved.

All rights reserved. No portion of this book may be reproduced, stored in a retrieval system, or transmitted in any form or by any means—electronic, mechanical, photocopy, recording, scanning, or otherwise—without prior written permission of the author.

Edited by Brad Shirley

Copyright © 2007 Pastor Leonard Gardner
All rights reserved.
ISBN: 1-4196-7797-7
ISBN-13: 978-1419677977

The Work of the Potter's Hands

Pastor Leonard Gardner

2007

The Work of the Potter's Hands

CONTENTS

Chapter 1—The Potter and the Clay	1
Chapter 2—The Process: Phase 1—Obtaining the Clay	7
Chapter 3—The Process: Phase 2—Preparing the Clay	11
Chapter 4—The Process: Phase 3—The Potter's Wheel	13
Chapter 5—The Process: Phase 4—Shaping the Clay	17
Chapter 6—The Process: Phase 5—The Sun and the Fire	25
Chapter 7—Vessels of Honor	31
Chapter 8—Vessels of Dishonor	37
Chapter 9—Broken Vessels	41
Chapter 10—Vessels of Wrath	49
Chapter 11—Clean Vessels	53
Chapter 12—Chosen Vessels	67
Chapter 13—Vessels of Mercy	79
Chapter 14—The Potter and You	85

CHAPTER 1

The Potter and the Clay

Jeremiah was one of the major prophets of the Old Testament, a man to whom God gave spiritual insights which many of the other prophets weren't privileged to experience. Jeremiah Chapter 18 speaks of a very significant time in the life and ministry of Jeremiah. He had already prophesied for many years, but God was preparing to take him to a new level. God wanted to give Jeremiah more anointing, more power, and more revelation. God was about to move Jeremiah *from the nominal to the phenomenal*. I believe that each of us has a desire in our hearts to be more than average, more than just "nominal." We each have a desire to live a life of meaning and purpose, and to be all that we were meant to be. In short, we each want to be phenomenal in some way. But how do we get from the nominal to the phenomenal? How do we become all that God intends for us to become? God answered that question for Jeremiah, and for us, by showing him an analogy of a potter and his work.

Jeremiah 18:1-2 declares, "The word which came to Jeremiah from the Lord, saying, Arise. Go down to the potter's house, and there I will cause thee to hear My words." Please note that God was the initiator. He was going to *cause* something to happen in Jeremiah. Also note that God didn't just want Jeremiah to hear His voice, but rather to hear His *words*. The Hebrew word *dabar*, which is used in that passage, literally means "words," which in turn implies "to know what He is saying." I believe, according to John's Gospel, that it is the birthright of all born again believers to know God's voice. Jesus said that His sheep know His voice. (John 10:4) Unfortunately, though, there are many people who don't know His words or what He is saying. *God wants us to not only hear His voice, but to understand what He is saying, and to understand what He means by what He says.* He wants us to have intimate knowledge of His character and His ways. God gave a special gifting to the sons of Issachar, one of the tribes of Israel. I Chronicles 12:32 declares, "And of the children of Issachar, which were men that had understanding of the times, to know what Israel ought to do." These men had an understanding of the times and they knew what Israel was supposed to do. Understanding and knowing are gifts from God. God was effectively saying to Jeremiah, "As I move you from the nominal to the phenomenal, you're going to progress from simply hearing my voice to the point of understanding my words and knowing what I meant by what I said." All babies immediately know the sound of their mother's voice, but there comes a time in the child's growth and development in which it becomes important that he or she not only hear and recognize Mom's voice, but also understand what Mom is saying. It is the same in our spiritual development. We must reach a place of spiritual maturity at which we begin to function at the level which God intended when He created us. Jeremiah was at this spiritual place in his life, and God was ready to take him to a higher level of spiritual maturity and usefulness. I believe that is where God is calling us and leading us today—higher in Him.

Jeremiah Chapter 18 continues, "Then I went down to the potter's house, and, behold, he wrought a work on the wheels. And the vessel that he made of clay was marred in the hand of the potter, so he made it again another vessel as it seemed good to the potter to make it." (Jeremiah 18:3-4) Note the phrase, "*as it seemed good to the potter.*" It doesn't say, "as it seemed good to the vessel." The image of what this vessel is going to be and the purpose that it is going to ultimately serve is in the mind of the <u>potter</u>. He communicates that mental image to his hands, because his hands actually touch and form the clay. His hands are responsive to his thoughts, and therefore the image of the vessel that he wants to make (its design, shape, size, and purpose) is already in the mind of the potter.

The Importance of the Potter

The Bible mentions the word "potter" twenty-two times, which suggests the importance that God places upon this subject. Isaiah 64:8 declares, "But now, O Lord, Thou art our father. We are the <u>clay</u>, and thou our <u>potter</u>." The subject of the potter is very relevant to us. The potter and his work are a type, an analogy, and a picture, given to help us understand our relationship with God and His plan for us. It is very important that we understand that He is the potter, and we are the clay. Some people struggle in their Christian walk because they have not wholly embraced this truth. I want to emphasize something right up front. <u>He is the potter</u>. <u>We are the clay</u>.

The second part of the verse states, "and we all are the work of thy hand." Please notice the word "all." *<u>Every one of us is the work of the potter's hand.</u>* Please note the last two words of the verse: "thy hand." All of us are "the work of Thy hand." We are not the work of a committee. The Hebrew word translated hand is *"yad,"* and it means your "open hand," which in turn means "the direction and the purpose that you have ordained." We are all the handiwork of the Lord. He is fashioning, designing, preparing, shaping, and "making" each of us, individually, according to His divine plan. First comes the plan, then comes the product. He is the potter; we are the clay. The potter has a plan as He takes the clay and fashions us into a finished product. The process of becoming a product is comprised of experiences and circumstances in our lives. We are formed and fashioned through the things we experience in life according to His plan, and His desire is to move us from the nominal to the phenomenal. Do you believe, as I do, that God is in complete control? Even when things come against us that threaten to destroy us, God can turn them around and bring good out of them. I have great peace in the assurance that He is on the throne and He is in control. He is sovereign. Therefore I am not fearful. I have confidence in Him.

The Potter, the Clay and the Process

If we are to understand the Christian life and properly relate to God, then we must understand the potter, the clay, and the process. There is a _Potter_ (Him), and _clay_ (us). Then, there is a _process_ that consists of experiences and circumstances as He performs His creative handiwork in our lives. He does this in order to bring about His purpose in each of our lives according to what He preordained for us before we were even born. He has always had a plan.

For a long time, I had the desire to observe the work of a skilled potter, particularly as it was performed back in Bible times. A number of years ago, my desire was fulfilled as I was blessed to see a live demonstration by a gifted potter. He gathered a small group together and demonstrated the pottery process step by step as it applied to Scripture. I took mental notes as I watched this incredible presentation. Many Bible truths came alive in me as I observed the potter doing his work.

I am excited to share with you some things I learned at that demonstration as well as some things that the Lord showed me in my personal study. A wonderful book entitled "The Potter's

Touch" by Sam Sasser was also a tremendous source of inspiration and information to me, particularly in my study of the seven different kinds of pottery vessels which are referred to in the Bible. I believe these truths will revolutionize your life. I have titled this book "The Work of the Potter's Hands," to emphasize that God lovingly created each of us and is committed to make of our lives what He intended. I wholeheartedly believe that He has a unique plan and purpose for each of us.

Seven Kinds of Vessels

In the Bible, pieces of pottery are called vessels. There are seven kinds of vessels which are identified in Scripture:
- vessels of honor,
- vessels of dishonor,
- broken vessels,
- vessels of wrath,
- clean vessels,
- chosen vessels, and
- vessels of mercy.

Each of these seven vessels had a unique function and place in the lives of people in Bible days. In this book, we will look at each of these types of vessels. We will learn what each vessel signifies, and in doing so it will help us to understand God's working in our own lives.

The more I study this subject and learn about it, the more my heart cries, "Oh God, make me everything You intend for me to be." I don't want to fall short of that. I realize that I can't "make" myself. Only God can make me, and I want to be yielded to Him. There is a "making process" that takes place from raw material to the finished product, and there are five major phases of that making process. Each of the seven kinds of vessels must go through this five-phase process. Each of us, as the work of the Potter's hands, must also go through a similar process as He lovingly and carefully forms us and takes us from the nominal to the phenomenal!

CHAPTER 2

The Process: Phase 1 Obtaining the Clay

Psalm 40:1 declares, "I waited patiently for the Lord, and He inclined unto me, and He heard my cry." Waiting on the Lord is where it all starts. Verse 2 states, "He brought me up also out of a horrible pit, out of the miry clay."

Phase one of the five-phase process begins when the potter obtains the clay with which to work. A potter in Bible days couldn't go to the store and buy clay. There were no malls or craft stores. He had to acquire the clay by his own effort, and he personally selected it himself. He acquired it by going to what was called the "pit," a large hole in the ground that was usually circular in shape, with very smooth walls. It was very deep and continually getting deeper as more clay was removed from it. The deeper it was, the darker it was. In the bottom of the pit, the only light that could be seen was by looking straight up. The pit was dark and slimy. It contained clay which was described in Psalm 40:2 as "miry," which means "muddy; mucky; gooey; slimy."

Although the pit was slimy, deadly, and dark, the best raw material (the most valuable and usable clay) was found in the very bottom of the pit. Similarly, when God prepared to make you and me, He obtained the "raw material" in the miry pit; the slimy, smelly, muddy, mucky pit. Clay can't get out of the pit by itself, and neither can we. If someone doesn't reach down into the pit and get the clay, it will never get out. If anyone fell into a pit, they cried loudly for help, hoping that someone was near enough to hear their cry, because there was no way to get out of the pit on their own. Psalm 40:1 declares that our cry is unto the Lord. We were the clay down in the bottom of the deep, dark pit of sin without any hope. There was no way for any of us to get out by ourselves. People try to build religious ladders to get out of the pit, but there is no way out unless Jesus hears our cry and lifts us out. Thank God that He hears our cry, and in His infinite mercy He reaches down, takes hold of us and says, "I am going to make something good out of this."

Whenever we sense pride or self-righteousness within us, we must remind ourselves of where we came from, and who lifted us out of there. Isaiah 51:1 effectively states, "Remember, don't ever forget the pit out of which you were dug." When that old, stinky flesh wants to rise up, we need to remember that Jesus found us in the pit.

What wonderful love, grace, and mercy God has for us that He would take the initiative to reach into the pit, rescue us, and give meaning to our lives. We didn't find God. He found us. (John 15:16) We simply responded to Him when He reached down with His nail-scarred hand, took hold of us, and pulled us out of the pit. He didn't see us as we were—mucky, slimy, and seemingly useless. Instead, He saw us as we could be. He loves us and has a purpose and a plan for every one of us.

But can any good thing come out of the pit? In Bible times, they looked at Jesus and they essentially asked the same question. Jesus was from Nazareth, which was a tiny town in the middle of nowhere. Nathaniel said, "Can any good thing come out of Nazareth?" (John 1:46) Yes, because when God gets hold of the mud and the clay, He makes something beautiful. He is not asking that we call ourselves muddy and mucky and constantly put ourselves down. It is true that when we are born again, we are indeed new creatures in Christ (II Corinthians 5:17), but we must keep a balanced view of ourselves. If we are going to stay humble and yielded, we must realize what we once were, and we must realize that God is the one who made us what we are today. All the glory is His. He is the only one that can make us what we were intended to be.

CHAPTER 3

The Process: Phase 2 Preparing the Clay

In the second phase of the process, the potter prepares the clay. Isaiah 41:25 gives us some insight into this phase: "I have raised up one from the north, and he shall come. From the rising of the sun shall he call upon My name. He shall come upon princes, as upon mortar, and <u>as the potter treadeth out the clay</u>."

In order to prepare the clay, the potter treads it out. He washes it and he begins to stomp and jump on it as hard as he can in order to get the air pockets out of the clay. After it begins to soften, he applies water to it to soften it even more. As it becomes more pliable, he kneads it, works on it with his hands, slaps it, and beats it. Before the live pottery demonstration which I observed, I could hear the potter preparing the clay backstage. I heard *pow, boom, boom, bap, bap*. The pounding was so intense that I thought, "If I was the clay, I would be calling 911!" We need not be discouraged if we feel like we are being pummeled, pounded, and tread upon. It may be that the Potter is preparing us for the next phase of His plan!

Bakers make bread "the old fashioned way" by kneading and working the dough, softening it, stretching it, rolling it, and pounding it with their fists. All of this work is done in order to prepare the dough so that it can become that wonderful finished product—fresh baked bread. During this sometime "violent" process, water must be added to bring the dough to the right consistency and make it pliable.

Likewise, a potter knows that the consistency must be just right in the mixture of the solid material and the water. If there is too much water, it will be too sloppy to shape. If there is not enough water, it will be too hard to be molded. In Ephesians 5:26, water is described as being symbolic of the Word of God. We all need the water of the Word applied to our lives to help prepare us to be all that God intends for us to be. Water is a very important part of the making process. Without water, dough couldn't become delicious bread, and clay couldn't become a beautiful and useful vessel. Likewise, without the water of the Word of God, we cannot become all that God intends for us to be.

As the potter prepares the clay, he is doing so with an image of the finished product in his mind, an image of the vessel he intends to create. During this preparation phase, the potter's primary goal is to prepare the clay mixture so that it can be placed on the potter's wheel for shaping. The preparation phase, though perhaps not particularly welcomed or invited, is extremely important in the overall process of making a beautiful and useful vessel.

CHAPTER 4

The Process: Phase 3
The Potter's Wheel

In phase three of the five-phase process, the potter places the softened clay on the potter's wheel. Psalm 40:2 declares, "He brought me up also out of an horrible pit, out of the miry clay. And <u>He set my feet upon a rock</u> and established my goings." The Hebrew word translated "established" means that He "fixed, determined, ordered, and ordained" what was going to happen to me.

Let me take a moment to describe for you the kind of potter's wheel that the skilled potter which I observed was using. There were two popular types of potter's wheels in Bible times, and the one which I saw was perhaps the most common type. The "wheel" actually consisted of two stone disks, though it was referred to as a singular "potter's wheel." On the bottom was a huge circular stone which weighed between four hundred and five hundred pounds. The potter would move this lower stone with his foot and leg, much like the motion you would make if you are running. The larger lower stone was connected by a wooden shaft to an upper stone which became the table upon which he worked. The upper stone was about half the size of the lower stone, approximately twenty-four inches in diameter. After preparing the clay, he began to move the lower wheel, which turned the upper wheel, and he then took the ball of clay and placed it on the upper stone.

The bottom of the vessel is called the "foot" of the vessel. Please see that what the potter did when he put the "foot" of the vessel on the rock was Scriptural. "He established my goings." (Psalm 40:2) The Potter took us out of the pit, He prepared us, and He placed us on the wheel. That's our story; out of the pit and onto the Rock. Jesus is the Rock!

Centered on the Rock

After the potter placed the glob of clay on the spinning rock, he placed his hands on the clay. As he put his hands on the clay, his hands began to shake. He said, "Do you know why my hands are shaking? It is because the clay is not *centered* on the rock. If it is not centered on the rock, it will fight my hands. It will resist what I want to do. It will do its own thing." Many of us have sung the hymn, "On Christ the Solid Rock I stand." It is not enough to be "on" the rock. We must be "centered on" the rock. We must be "Christocentric," that is, Christ-centered. Unfortunately, many people are centered on a lot of other things.

When we are born into this world, we are *eccentric*, which means off-center. As we grow, we begin to listen to the teachings of the secular education system, and we can become *egocentric*, meaning "centered on ourselves." This is the thought that essentially implies "it's all about us," that God may be out there somewhere, but life is all about us. Or, we can become *polycentric*, which means we have more than one center. James 1:8 states that a double-minded man (a polycentric man) is "unstable in all his ways." Also, the enemy often works to draw us into becoming *geocentric*, that is, centered on the things of this world. Philippians 3:19 speaks of those who "mind earthly things."

Instead, we need to be Christocentric! Simply being religious or going to church isn't enough because even religious people can get centered on doctrines, preachers, churches, ministries, messages, or gifts. It seems easy to become centered on everything but Jesus.

When the lump of clay is not centered on the rock, the master potter has trouble. He simply can't continue to form the vessel until it gets centered. If he tries to shape the vessel before it is centered, one side of the vessel will become thick and the other side will become thin. The result of the thick side pressing upon the thin side will produce stress that will crack the vessel. That is the definition, in my opinion, of a "crackpot"—one who is "not centered on Jesus."

In order to get the clay centered, the potter speeds up the wheel. There are no markings on the upper stone to indicate to the potter that the clay is centered on the rock. How then does the potter know when the clay is centered? *He knows it's centered when the clay stops resisting him.* He keeps his hands on the clay, and the more he speeds the wheel up, the less it resists his hands. When it quits fighting him, he knows it is centered. Many people have not come into the fullness of God's purpose for their life because they are not centered on Jesus. They are still resisting the Potter's hand, struggling against His purpose and plan, and they are therefore unhappy, unfulfilled, and devoid of the blessings of the Lord.

This process of moving from being raw material to being centered on the rock is vital to the next phase, which is the shaping and molding phase. The potter won't begin the shaping and molding until the clay is centered. He doesn't want to produce crackpots. He wants to produce whole, beautiful, useful vessels. We must be centered on Jesus the Rock!

CHAPTER 5

The Process: Phase 4 Shaping the Clay

In the fourth phase of the process, the potter shapes the clay. The clay is now lying as a glob centered on the potter's wheel, ready for the potter to shape it. In essence, the potter now begins to bring some meaning to this pile of clay. It is called the process of shaping.

I am absolutely convinced that when God calls each of us, reaching into the miry clay and pulling us out, He has a purpose and a plan in mind. He doesn't just pull us out and look at the glob and say, "Why did I do that?" He had the plan in mind before He reached for the glob. The Potter doesn't turn to the clay and ask, "What would you like to be? Do you have a desire?" He doesn't turn to another vessel that is already made and ask, "What would you like Me to do with this glob?" He doesn't need advice. He, and He alone, has the plan. He has the plan according to His intended use for the vessel.

There are different kinds of pottery. Some vessels contain liquid and are used to pour into other vessels. Another kind of vessel, although it can also contain and pour, has a different kind of lip because it is intended to be used as a drinking vessel. The potter has a unique shape in mind when he begins. He knows what purpose each vessel is going to serve.

Ephesians 4:11 declares that when Jesus "ascended on high,

He led captivity captive, and He gave gifts unto men. And He gave some, <u>apostles</u>; and some, <u>prophets</u>; and some, <u>evangelists</u>; and some, <u>pastors</u> and <u>teachers</u>." This is known as the fivefold ministry because there are five ministry gifts listed: apostles, prophets, evangelists, pastors and teachers. Why did He give us this fivefold ministry? He did it "For the perfecting of the saints." (Ephesians 4:12) The word "perfecting" means "molding, shaping, and making into what it is intended to be; whole, complete, mature." He perfects the saints "for the work of the ministry, for the edifying of the body of Christ." Ultimately, He wants us to minister to other people, and He wants that to occur through the work of the ministry as everyone does their appointed part. Some people have the God-given gifts to function as an evangelist, some are gifted to be a pastor, and so on. We must learn to receive ministry from each of these kinds of ministers, who each play an important part in the overall plan of God.

A Fivefold Analogy

The human hand is a good example of the fivefold ministry of Ephesians 4:11. Just as the clay is formed in the hands of the potter, the Lord takes our lives, and through the fivefold ministry that He has given to the Church, He molds and shapes us as we are responsive and yielded to Him.

The thumb represents the <u>apostle</u>. The thumb is very fundamental to the whole hand. It is the most flexible digit and it works with every finger in the hand. You can pick something up with a thumb and any finger. It is a basic and extremely functional part of the hand.

The first finger, which we call the index finger, is the "pointer." It shows direction and purpose. That represents the <u>prophet</u>. The prophet gives the word of direction and guidance.

The next finger, the longest finger, represents the <u>evangelist</u>. It represents outreach. It goes beyond all the other fingers. It touches what the others can't touch, and represents the heart and ministry of the evangelist.

The next finger, which we call the ring finger, represents the <u>pastor</u>. This is the only finger of the five that has a vein connected directly from it all the way to the heart. That is why we put the ring on that finger. It represents covenant love. The pastor is to have a heart for people. He is to be a shepherd, a keeper of the sheep.

The little finger is very important as well. It represents the <u>teacher</u>. It is the probing finger. It is the one that gets us in trouble many times, just like a teacher, who is the prober, seeker, and extractor of information.

In a spiritual sense, let us "see" the hands of our Lord Jesus Christ holding the clay as He ministers to us. In the same way that the clay responds to the physical hand of the potter, we must respond to all five fingers of the spiritual hand of Jesus, His fivefold ministry. We must be open and responsive to the ministry of the apostle, prophet, evangelist, pastor, and teacher. Some people say, "I only listen to God." Well, God speaks and works through people also. Yes, God can and does speak directly to us at times, but He has given His "spiritual hand" (the fivefold ministry) to show us that He can and does speak to us more often through others. I Peter 5:6 declares, "Humble yourselves therefore under the mighty hand of God, that He may exalt you in due time."

Upward Pressure!

As I watched the potter begin to do his work on the glob of clay, I noticed that the first thing that he did was apply pressure to it. We may say, "I hate pressure. Pray for me, that I can get free of pressure." However, pressure is vital to maintaining life. If you have ever flown on an airplane you know that. Before a plane takes off, the flight attendant will say something like, "The cabin is pressurized. We can't go higher unless we take pressure with us. If something happens which causes us to lose cabin pressure, an oxygen mask will drop down. You must put it on if you want to continue to breathe." When we send astronauts into space, we pressurize their spacecraft and their spacesuits because they couldn't survive without pressure. These analogies teach us that we can't function in a higher place without pressure. As God works in our lives to bring meaning, shape and purpose to this "glob of clay," pressure is an important part of the process. We must be aware that the pressure is applied by the gentle nail-scarred hands of the Potter. At times, we all need pressure, because we all may find ourselves getting off center. Thank God that He loves us so much that He applies pressure to get us back to being centered on Jesus.

As the potter is shaping a vessel, he begins to mold it by applying pressure on the outside. The pressure is what defines the shape. Without pressure, a vessel could never have a lip. Without pressure, a vessel can't be properly shaped so that it can be gripped and used. Vessels would be useless if it were not for the gentle pressure and molding of the potter.

It is interesting that the potter's hands are always moving in an upward direction as he applies the pressure and shapes the vessel. He never pushes downward on it. He puts his hands on the glob of clay at the bottom of the wheel and he gives it shape and meaning by working it in an upward direction. This is a beautiful picture of how God, as He works in our lives, always moves us upward in life. He never pushes us down or brings harm or condemnation to us. His purpose is always to draw us to Himself, to lift us higher, to shape us, and to mold us. When we are on the Potter's wheel and we are feeling the pressure, we should be encouraged, because He is moving us upward. He is applying *upward pressure* to our life. The pressure is going to take us in an upward direction, closer to God's purpose and plan for our life.

The Heart

As I watched the potter beginning to bring shape to the glob of clay, I noticed that the clay began to look attractive, and I began to imagine its ultimate shape and intended usefulness. Then he said, "Now I must do something that seems cruel," and he took his fingers and forced them right down into the center of the vessel. He said, "I must work on the inside, which is called the 'heart.'" The potter said, "If I don't work on the heart, it can never contain anything, and consequently it will never be able to pour anything." If the potter doesn't work on the heart, the vessel *looks* useful, but with no inside opening, it is *not* useful. The bigger it is inside, the more it can contain and the more it can pour. Scripture speaks of the enlarged heart (Psalm 119:32). Enlarge us God, so that we can hold more, and therefore pour more out.

Many people are only concerned about the way they look on the outside. Jesus isn't too concerned with how we look. He is concerned about what we can give. When He took us from the miry clay, His intention was to make givers out of us, not just receivers, not just something that is attractive on the outside. His intention was to make us useful, because beauty without usefulness makes a vessel valueless. I could hold a cup, but if it had no opening on the inside, it wouldn't serve me because I couldn't take a drink of water from it. I couldn't be refreshed unless something happened to its heart. I could only taste whatever ran off the outside. The heart is very important in the making process. In I Samuel 16:7, the prophet Samuel declared, "Man looketh on the outward appearance, but God looketh on the heart."

The potter said to all of us, "Please take note of something else. None of you out there can see the heart of this vessel. You must get close to the potter to see it." As he plunged his fingers down into the heart of the vessel, soon His whole hand was in there. He had one hand on the inside and one hand on the outside. That is what I call "working on the whole man." God not only works on our body and our soul, but also on our spirit. He is doing something that is critical to our usefulness. We can't pour more than we can contain. We may say, "Don't mess around with me too much, Lord, but really use me. God, really anoint me, but don't alter my lifestyle. Don't rearrange my priorities or my value system. Remove Your hand from my heart." We want to be used, but in order to be *greatly* used, the Potter must work *deeply* in our hearts.

The Mouth

After the potter has shaped and molded the vessel both inwardly and outwardly, he must finish with the topmost part, which is called the "mouth." God took us from the miry clay, and He put our feet on the rock. He is now working on our heart, and He is shaping our mouth. Scripture declares, "Out of the abundance of the heart, the mouth speaketh." (Matthew 12:34) What comes out of our mouth is what is in our heart. That is why the heart is so very important, and that is why Proverbs 4:23 declares that we need to guard our heart. If the heart gets contaminated, dirty, and unclean, whatever comes out of it will be unclean. Regardless of how attractive the vessel may appear, its contents, and therefore what it pours, will be impure and contaminated. When we allow our hearts to become hardened or rebellious and we start murmuring, gossiping, complaining, or criticizing, we can't pour forth good things. James 3:10 states that blessing and cursing cannot come out of the same mouth. It is either filled with one or the other. The way that we guard our mouth is by guarding our heart. If we start to hear things come out of our *mouth* that shouldn't be coming out, we should ask God to work on our *heart*, because there must be something wrong in the heart, something that has not been dealt with. We can have shape and beauty and look useful, yet be useless. If I am a thirsty man and I look at a beautiful vessel, I envision cold water to quench my thirst. But if the vessel doesn't contain something which quenches my thirst, it can bring poison to my very being. Jesus, help us not to pour poison out of our mouths. Help us to guard our hearts.

Always in His Hands

Throughout the demonstration, the clay never left the hands of the potter. He had his hands on it the entire time with one notable and important exception. Occasionally, the potter would take one hand off the clay, get a handful of water, and then apply the water to the clay.

There are two significant symbolic truths here. First, please realize that <u>*the potter keeps his hands on the clay*</u>. He doesn't allow it to spin out of control or fall into a useless and formless glob. He is in control all the time. He keeps his hands on the clay, gently and patiently forming it. He never leaves it alone. Sometimes we think we are alone and nobody understands. Sometimes we think what we are going through is almost more than any human can bear. Oh, how important it is to look up and to see the nail-scarred hand of the Potter on our lives and be assured it is going to be okay. We are always in His hands!

A second important truth is that *the potter applies water periodically to the clay*. We know that water is a type of the Word of God. When the Potter has His hands on us, He will be faithful to keep the promises He has made in His Word, and He wants us to apply His Word and get it down deep into the very core of our being.

If we understand that the Potter has us in His hands at all times, and that He is applying His Word to our lives, it will help us to appreciate the reason God allows certain things to come into our lives that shape and mold us. A well-known hymn says it best. "Have Thine own way, Lord; have Thine own way. Thou art the Potter; I am the clay. Mold me and make me after Your will, while I am waiting, yielded and still."

CHAPTER 6

The Process: Phase 5
The Sun and the Fire

In phase 5, the potter must expose the newly formed vessel to intense heat. During the demonstration, the potter stopped the wheel and said, "This looks nice, doesn't it?" The audience replied, "Yes." He replied, "The problem is, if you try to take hold of this vessel, it will fall apart. It looks good, but it isn't strong yet." Therefore, the first thing that he does with a newly formed vessel is place it in the sun for a period of time. He called it the "s-u-n." I call it the "S-o-n." During this time, 30 percent of the water content in it evaporates. This water was only useful at the time it was being molded, and now it must be eliminated because the vessel must now take on stability and harden. After this evaporation takes place, the potter picks up the vessel and moves it to the oven (called a "kiln"), placing it into the twenty-four hundred degree heat of the fire. All of the very minute particles are fused together by the heat, and they become inseparable. There is a cohesiveness that results, and it brings strength to the vessel that it would not otherwise have had without the heat of the fire. Vessels only reach this "fire phase" if they have yielded to the shaping and surrendered to the hand of the potter and the work of the wheel.

I Peter 4:12 declares, "Don't think it strange, considering the fiery trial which is to try you, as though some strange thing happened unto you." Mr. Vessel, please understand that you were shaped to go into the fire. In fact, Peter said that we should not only accept the fact that this is normal, but we should actually rejoice in the fire! We might say, "Peter, now you have gone too far!" Not so. The next verse continues, "Inasmuch as you are partakers of Christ's sufferings, that when His glory shall be revealed, you may be glad also with exceeding joy." This is not referring to heaven, but rather right here on earth. Why are you exceedingly glad? Because you are able to be used for the purpose for which you were made! At the demonstration, the potter said, "If I don't put this vessel in the fire, it only has enough strength to hold itself up." It has the strength to stand on its own feet, but it can't minister to anybody else. I can't pour from the vessel or drink from the vessel unless it goes through the fire. If it hasn't been through the fire, the cup is attractive but not useful. Therefore, despite its attractiveness, it is not serving the purpose or the intent for which it was created until it goes through the fire.

The cry of my heart is that God will help us to understand. Many times as a pastor, I have looked into the casket of someone that has passed away and thought, "Lord, they had such potential for You." But too often they had pursued their own plan and charted their own course. In the same manner, we too often seem determined to do our own thing. We have established our own priorities and our own value system independent of Him. We are determined to attain this and obtain that, and to do this or do that, but the consequence is that we never become what God intended us to be when He pulled us out of the miry clay.

The Product is the Result of the Process

We become the product as a result of the process. Why did God do it that way? Why is there a process at all? Why didn't He just create vessels instead of creating clay? He could have done that.

He can do anything. When Jesus was teaching the disciples, He said to them, "Throw the net on the right side." Why did He have to go through all of that? Jesus could have just spoken to the fish and said, "Get in the boat, already deboned and filleted." However, God wants us to be active participants in His plan. The disciples were privileged to pull the net in. Jesus blessed them by including them in the process.

There is no limit to what Jesus can do. The working of His hand is to bring forth a product for the glory of His name, until our original "glob" isn't even recognizable anymore. We often make the mistake of trying to get our hands on the clay. We tend to try to push His hands out of the way, as if to say, "Hey, Jesus, I have an idea. Let's put a little groove right here. I want to be groovier." Can we just let go and trust Him? Can we trust the One that reached down into that dark pit and chose us when we were just a slimy glob of clay?

Marred In the Hand of the Potter

The entire five-phase making process can often be challenging and even difficult for the vessel. Sometimes, things don't go exactly as the Potter or the clay had intended. Jeremiah 18:4 declares, "The vessel that He made was marred in the hand of the potter. And he made it again another vessel." Note that the vessel was not marred *by* the hand the potter, but rather *in* the hand of the potter. The potter never mars a vessel, but sometimes the experiences, situations, circumstances, and affairs of this life "mar" us while we are in His hands in the making process. While the potter had the vessel, while he owned it, it became marred in his hand. Even though it became marred, the potter did not reject it. He made it *again* *another* vessel! He made it *again*. He took it out of the furnace, and if it was cracked, he would make it *again*. The word "again" is very vital to understanding the merciful heart of the potter.

Did he look at the marred vessel and say, "This isn't the way I intended it. This has a defect and it will never be useful to the extent I have ordained it?" No. Did he discard it, get more clay, and start over? No. Neither did he disown it or set it in the corner and say, "I am not proud of this vessel. It just didn't come out right." We, as humans, often do that to things that we make that don't turn out quite right. For example, I always cut boards too short. (Just at one end though).

What did the potter do when the vessel was marred? "He made it again." How many times is *again*? In my opinion, <u>*again* is one more time than it was marred</u>. One more time, the vessel is remade. I like that about God. Things that start off in darkness end up in light. Things that start off in death end up in life. Things that start off marred end up made whole again. I like that word "again." He doesn't say "a second time," or even "a seventh time." He simply says "again."

Perhaps you are thinking, "I have become a 'crackpot.'" I have slipped off center. I have resisted God's hands. I haven't allowed Him to work on my heart." He is saying to you, "Come back to Me. I will do it *again*." What a powerful illustration of the mercy and grace of God. He won't quit until the vessel finally becomes what He intended it to be.

The Twofold Purpose of the Process: To Minister and To Offer

God is a God of purpose. Everything He does is calculated to bring about a predefined purpose. What then is the purpose for the "making process" of a vessel? I believe that there is a twofold purpose, and it is revealed in II Chronicles 24:14, which declares, "And when they had finished it, they brought the rest of the money before the king and Jehoiada, whereof were made vessels for the house of the LORD, even <u>vessels to minister</u>, and to <u>offer</u> withal, and spoons, and vessels of gold and silver. And they offered burnt offerings in the house of the LORD continually all the days of Jehoiada."

Please note the twofold purpose: 1) "vessels to minister," and 2) "to offer." The word "minister" is translated from the Hebrew word *shareth*, and it means "to serve." It speaks of our horizontal responsibility to one another. The word "offer" in translated from the Hebrew word *alah,* and it means "to cause to go up." It speaks of our vertical responsibility to God. Therefore, the reason He makes us vessels is twofold. He wants us to <u>serve</u> one another and to <u>offer up</u> praise and thanksgiving to Him. The "ministry" and the "offering up" are *both* important.

Jesus, please touch our hearts once again. We try to run our own lives, program our own walk, and order our own steps. When things don't go our way, we tend to get irritated and angry. We fight Your hand so often, Lord, and then we wonder as we pray, "God, why don't You use us more? Why don't You anoint us more?" You tell us that somewhere along the line we have been marred. Perhaps we were marred because of what someone said or did to us, or perhaps something simply didn't turn out the way we had hoped or dreamed it would. We thought we were in control, and Jesus simply had to remind us through our experiences that we are not in control. He is.

It is time we bring our cracked, broken, and marred vessel back to the Potter and say, "Lord, I can't make this life what it ought to be, but I can bring it to You." Pray, "Dear Potter, make me again. Make me again, whatever it takes. I am frustrated with trying to do it on my own. I have failed. I have missed the mark. I have come up short. Now I yield myself to You." This is between you and God. Bring your "vessel" and place it back into the Potter's hands and say, "Lord, please continue Your purposeful work in my life."

CHAPTER 7

Vessels of Honor

Romans 9:20 states, "Nay but O man, who art thou that repliest against <disputes with> God? Shall the thing formed say to him that formed it, 'Why hast thou made me thus?'" In the Greek language, this isn't a question of inquiry, but rather a question of dispute. In other words, it is actually a question of criticism, as in, "God, why did You make me this way?" God gives us a little insight in verse 21, which states, "Hath not the potter power over the clay?" In other words, who is Lord? The Potter is the master, and the clay is not! Romans 9 continues, "And of the same lump to make one vessel unto honor and another unto dishonor?" God is asking a question in return. First, man questions God, effectively criticizing how God has made him. God gives His answer in question form, effectively saying, "Do not I have the power to make vessels as I choose to make them, whether I choose to make a vessel unto honor or choose to make a vessel unto dishonor?"

The Water Jar Bench

Near the entrance of every house, and also inside the entrance to the temple, was a bench about three to four feet high, called the "water jar bench," on which were set three vessels. There were two large vessels, one on either end of the bench, and one smaller vessel in the middle. One of the large vessels was a vessel of honor, and the other one was a vessel of dishonor. The third vessel, the smaller one, was used as a drinking cup. The water jar bench was a very common sight and a significant part of the lifestyle of the people of that day.

Vessels of Honor

The first vessel, called the "vessel of honor," was often cone-shaped. The top was a little smaller than the bottom, and it had an open mouth and open lip. Two handles were attached to the neck of the vessel. A chosen vessel usually contained about five gallons of water and was one of the more costly vessels. A potter took a great deal of time to make this kind of vessel. It not only had to be properly shaped but it also had to have handles attached and be thoroughly baked so that it was strong enough to carry five gallons of water. Every household would have one of these, though it was probably one of the most expensive vessels in their house.

The vessel of honor was used to fulfill a very important purpose. When someone came to another's house to visit, the guest stopped at the door and the host poured water from this vessel onto the guest's feet to cleanse them. In that day, the roads were very dusty and dirty, and people wore open sandals that were basically just leather pads strapped to the bottom of their feet.

In the temple, people would pour water on their feet and hands before they prayed. They believed that it was important to enter into the house of the Lord and into prayer with clean hands. Psalm 24:3 speaks literally of that, and also has spiritual interpretation and application: "Who shall ascend unto the hill of the Lord? And who shall stand in His holy place? He that hath clean hands and a pure heart, who has not lifted up his soul unto vanity nor sworn deceitfully." The vessel of honor was therefore used to wash their feet and their hands.

Water for the Thirsty

A third, and even more important, use for the vessel of honor was to provide water for the thirsty. They poured water from the vessel of honor into a smaller vessel, and then drank from the smaller vessel. The vessel of honor was always available to provide guests with water as a sign of hospitality. When people went to the temple, the water in the vessel of honor was always available to quench their thirst. People walked for miles in those times, so they frequently needed the refreshment that water provided. The vessel of honor was significant, both at the home and in the temple.

At least once a day, a householder took the vessel of honor to the well or brook to fill it with fresh water. It was the source of life for that entire day, and it provided nourishment, refreshment, and cleansing. This fresh water was essential for people to live in health and strength, and to be able to fulfill their daily responsibilities. This is pictured many times in the Bible. For example, in John Chapter 4, Jesus sat down at the well and waited until the woman from Samaria came to draw water. She was coming to fill the vessel of honor to meet the needs of that day.

It was considered unacceptable to deny anyone a drink of water. If someone passed you on the road and asked for a drink, it was expected that you would give them a drink without hesitation or question. If someone came to your home, they could get a drink. If someone walked by your home, they were welcome to take the vessel of honor and pour themselves a cup of water and drink it. Though the vessel belonged to the householder, the water in the vessel belonged to whoever asked for it. Everyone was welcome to it. A vessel of honor was always a welcome sight in a home and in the temple for anyone that needed a drink of water. They didn't have to pay for it nor earn it. It was there as an expression of love, available to all that were in need of it.

Fresh Water

I believe the same should be true in the spiritual realm. I believe that God sets people in His church who are vessels of honor. Who are they? They are the ones that go to the well every day and draw fresh spiritual water. They draw this fresh water by going to the Lord, the Well of Life, every day through prayer, Bible study and meditation, and in personal times of fellowship and worship. God is the only Source of this life-giving water.

When you see these vessels of honor or cross their path, you receive something refreshing and cool. Jesus alluded to Himself in John 7:37 as a vessel of honor. He said, "If any man thirst, let him come unto Me and drink." He was effectively saying, "I am available. I offer you fresh water." It is not day-old water. It is fresh water. Some people try to pour fresh water, yet they only draw it once a week (in church on Sunday), and it becomes stale and stagnant. Water must be drawn every day from the cool of the well. It must be fresh.

I thank God for the vessels of honor that are available. When we have a need, a problem, or something that requires prayer, we call a vessel of honor. We call someone that has been to the well. I trust that you go to the well even before you attend church. Don't just go to church as if it is the well itself. You should get to the well (God) and then go to church with a vessel full of water. Go ready to pour, give, and bless. I Corinthians 14:26 states, "How is it then, brethren? When ye come together, every one of you hath a psalm, hath a doctrine, hath a tongue, hath a revelation, hath an interpretation. Let all things be done unto edifying." Let each one of us come with something to <u>give</u>!

We tend to have a consumer mentality in that we go to church only to receive, but we have it backwards. Please don't go to church and expect your pastor or someone else to pour water into your vessel. You should be obtaining your water at the same place where your pastor and leaders get their water—the Well of Life. You should be going to the well multiple times a day, every day. If your supply gets used up by noon, go back to the well. Open your Bible and spend some time in prayer or worship. Can you imagine what would happen in your community if everyone in your church were vessels of honor, full every day with water from the well? God wants vessels of honor. You can be a vessel of honor, full of the refreshing, life-giving Word of God!

If you are tired, weary, weak or sick, and you are walking down the road past a house and see such a vessel of honor, say "Thank God," take hold of it and drink. You don't even have to ask, because it belongs to you. It belongs to everyone that will receive. You don't have to knock at the door. You don't have to pay a price. Oh, that God would make such willing and available vessels of each of us!

CHAPTER 8

Vessels of Dishonor

A vessel of dishonor was the large vessel at the other end of the water jar bench. The vessel of dishonor was so named because it was flawed at some point in the making process. Possibly, there was too much air in the clay, or perhaps the clay was very gritty or had hard lumps in it such that the potter could not make it the perfect vessel that he intended. In other words, the failure was not on the part of the potter, but rather on the part of the clay. We learned earlier that if the clay wasn't centered on the wheel, one side of the vessel would be thicker than the other and the resulting stress would cause the pot to crack. Cracked pots were sold at a very cheap price and were frequently purchased by householders. They not only didn't have the shape of the vessel of honor, but they didn't have the purpose of the vessel of honor.

Vessels of Dishonor

These cracked vessels had a different usage. They were used to hold stale and dirty water. Also, when a meal was over, people took the plates and scraped the dregs into this vessel. You might say, and accurately so, that this vessel was a garbage can. You can imagine, being used as such, that it wasn't long before its contents would become very putrid and begin to draw flies. After it was full of garbage and was giving off an unpleasant odor, the householder would simply take it out to the dung hill and throw away both the contents and the vessel itself. Once it had been thrown on the dung hill, it was then called an "abominable" vessel. A vessel of dishonor became an abominable vessel (Isaiah 65:4) when it was discarded because it wasn't of any further use, even as a garbage can.

The shape of a vessel of dishonor was significantly different than the shape of a vessel of honor. Again, the bottom of the vessel was called the "foot," the inside was called the "heart," and the top was called the "mouth." When dregs, putrid water, and dead flies are inside, the heart of the vessel is full of death. When the heart is full of death and not cleansed, it is abominable. "Throw it away. Go get another one. They are cheap. Go back to the potter and purchase another one."

I don't want to be a vessel that is available to collect slop and garbage. Eventually, a vessel in that condition attracts many flies. The Bible tells us one of the names of the enemy is "Beelzebub," which means "the lord of the flies." The spiritual analogy is that, as vessels who allow ourselves to collect ungodly and unhealthy things, we can drift away from God and allow the devil to have his way. We can become useless and abominable. Gossip and discord are typical of things that we can collect in our vessel if we aren't careful. Recorded in Proverbs 6:16, God declares, "There are six things I hate, and the seventh is an abomination unto Me, he that soweth discord among the brethren."

Charles Allen, in his book *God's Psychiatry*, wrote, "Great minds discuss ideas. Mediocre minds discuss events. Small minds discuss people." Guarding our attitude and controlling our tongue is vital to avoid becoming a vessel of dishonor.

Hope for the Dishonorable

For a long time, I labored over Romans 9:21, and I prayed, "God, I don't understand. In that Scripture, You said some are made vessels of honor and some dishonor. Are You saying that some people are irrevocably vessels of dishonor? Are You saying that some are created to be dishonorable, and there is no way they can ever change? Are You saying they are always going to be that way?" Then the Lord revealed something to me found in II Timothy 2:20-21 that really encouraged me.

The Apostle Paul wrote to his spiritual son Timothy and stated, "But in a great house there are not only vessels of gold and of silver, but also of wood and of earth, some to honor and some to dishonor." Note the word "if" in II Timothy 2:21: "If a man therefore purge himself from these, he shall be a vessel unto honor, sanctified and meet for the master's use and prepared unto every good work." <u>If a man purge himself, he shall be</u>. When we are born in the natural, as the seed of Adam, we have an inclination, a tendency, toward being a dishonorable vessel. But thank God that we need not remain a vessel of dishonor. There is something we can do about it! It is conditional. By nature, we are vessels of dishonor, but we can become vessels of honor, going to the well daily and supplying life. What do we have to do in order to become a vessel of honor once again? Let's read on.

II Timothy 2:22-26 declares, "Flee youthful lusts, follow righteousness, faith, charity, peace, with them that call on the Lord out of a pure heart. But foolish and unlearned questions avoid, knowing that they do gender strifes. And the servant of the Lord must not strive, but be gentle unto all men, apt to teach, patient, in meekness instructing those that oppose themselves if God peradventure will give them repentance to the acknowledging of the truth and that they may recover themselves out of the snare of the devil, who are taken captive by him at his will."

The Apostle Paul is saying that there are some that are in opposition because they have been taken captive by the devil, but the servant of the Lord (the vessel of honor) must be patient and instruct these people, believing that God will call them to repentance and turn them around. He told us to avoid strife, as well as the other things listed in II Timothy Chapter 2, if we want to be a vessel of honor. II Timothy 2 brings clarity to Romans 9, and clearly states that it is not God's ordained purpose that any of us be vessels of dishonor. In fact, Jeremiah 18:4 shows us that when we are flawed in the process of the making, He will put us back on the wheel and make us whole again.

A Prayer to the Potter

Father, it is with hearts of thanksgiving that we acknowledge what You have done for us. We examine our own hearts before You, Lord. May it be said of each of us that we are vessels of honor, not because we are perfect or without flaw, but because we have learned the secret of going to the well every day and drawing water, and because we have refused to be collectors and containers of dregs, dirty water and garbage. Cleanse us and purify us. Have Your own way, Lord. You are the Potter; we are the clay. Lord, if there are any cracks in our vessel; if there are any stones, grit, or anything else that has resisted Your hand and Your shaping, we invite You to put us back on the wheel. Make us into vessels of honor for Your glory.

CHAPTER 9

Broken Vessels

In Psalm 31, David expressed his confidence in God in spite of the fact that he was in a great deal of trouble. He was in trouble for two reasons: 1) there were people that didn't like him, and 2) he saw things in himself that he didn't like. Can you identify with that? David cried unto the Lord (Psalm 31:1-9), "In Thee, O Lord, do I put my trust; let me never be ashamed. Deliver me in Thy righteousness. Bow down Thine ear to me; deliver me speedily. Be Thou my strong rock, for a house of defense to save me. Thou art my rock and my fortress; therefore, for Thy name's sake lead me and guide me. Pull me out of the net that they have laid privily for me, for Thou art my strength. Into Thine hand I commit my spirit: Thou hast redeemed me, O Lord God of truth. I have hated them that regard lying vanities, but I trust in the Lord. I will be glad and rejoice in Thy mercy, for Thou hast considered my trouble." God always considers our troubles! "Thou hast known my soul in adversities and hast not shut me up into the hand of the enemy. Thou hast set my feet in a large room. Have mercy upon me, O Lord, for I am in trouble." Have you ever prayed a similar prayer?

David continues in Psalm 31, "Mine eye is consumed with grief, yea, my soul and my belly. My life is spent with grief, and my years with sighing. My strength faileth because of mine iniquity" (please note that David speaks of his own iniquity) "and my bones are consumed. I was a reproach among all mine enemies but especially among my neighbors, and a fear to mine acquaintance. They that did see me without fled from me. I am forgotten as a dead man out of mind."

David the Broken Vessel

In Psalm 31:12, David writes, "I am like a broken vessel. For I have heard the slander of many. Fear was on every side. While they took counsel together against me, they devised to take away my life. But I trusted in Thee, O Lord: I said, 'Thou art my God.' My times are in Thy hand. Deliver me from the hand of mine enemies and from them that persecute me. Make Thy face to shine upon Thy servant and save me for Thy mercies' sake. Let me not be ashamed, O Lord, for I have called upon Thee. Let the wicked be ashamed, and let them be silent in the grave. Let the lying lips be put to silence, which speak grievous things proudly and contemptuously against the righteous. Oh, great is Thy goodness, which Thou hast laid up for them that fear Thee, which Thou hast wrought for them that trust in Thee before the sons of men! Thou shalt hide them in the secret of they presence from the pride of man, and Thou shalt keep them secretly in a pavilion from the strife of tongues. Blessed be the Lord, for He hath showed me His marvelous kindness in a strong city. For I said in my haste, 'I am cut off from before Thine eyes.' Nevertheless, Thou heardest the voice of my supplications when I cried unto Thee. Oh love the Lord, all ye His saints, for the Lord preserveth the faithful, and plentifully rewardeth the proud doer. Be of good courage, and He shall strengthen your heart, all ye that hope in the Lord."

David, as a type (a symbol) of the born again believer, walked through many of the things that we face and, in Psalm 31, he shows us a picture of the broken vessel. We must understand God's commitment to the broken vessel—to mend it and make it whole—and the process that He uses to mend that which is broken.

A "broken vessel" is defined as one of two things. It is defined as either a vessel which has been marred in the process of being used (dropped, chipped, or otherwise marred), or one that could not or would not take the fire in the fifth phase in the making process. Some vessels resist the heat, and they crack. In summary, <u>*a broken vessel is either one that was cracked in the process of the making or marred in the process of the using.*</u>

In Bible times when a vessel was broken, it wasn't discarded. People weren't careless with a broken vessel. They took it back to the potter to be mended, and he used a very special process, which included blood and fire, to repair the vessel.

The Mending Process: Blood and Fire

First, the potter would prepare a substance that consisted of dry powder clay. Secondly, he went out into the fields and gathered small tick-like insects called *fasukas*. He gathered several at a time, putting them into a jar and keeping them to use in mending vessels. He found these little fasukas in the hair on the backs of bulls and goats, and he put them in his container until the time of vessel mending. When it came time to make a vessel new again, he opened the container and took one of the little fasukas out. He held it over the dry powder clay and squeezed it between his thumb and his forefinger. As he did that, the blood of the fasuka flowed down into the clay. The potter then mixed the blood with the clay, and it became a glue-like, paste-like substance. The blood of the fasuka possessed a cohesive quality such that when it was mixed with clay, it caused the clay to be fused. The potter used the mixture to mold, remold, and repair the vessel.

After he made the repair, he took the vessel and put it back into the fire again, right back into the same fire out of which it had come. In some cases, this vessel may have been marred in the process of using, but in other cases it was marred in the fire itself. It may have been a vessel that cracked while it was being fired. When this happened, the potter took it out of the fire, and with the blood of the fasuka and dry clay, he mended the crack and then again put it right back into the same fire. Sometimes it cracked again. When it cracked, the potter, in a very patient and dedicated manner, would repeat the process of mixing more dry clay and fasuka blood, mending it, and placing it back into the fire again.

Sometimes he spent hours mending the vessel. He was very patient, because the vessel was very important to him. He had made the vessel, and he wanted it to retain the same shape that it had when it was new. He repeated the mending process, as often as necessary, until he had dealt with all the cracked and broken areas.

The Importance of the Blood

Let's apply this to our own personal life. In the same way that the blood of the fasuka was very important in mending the broken vessel and making it whole again, so the blood of Jesus is very important to us. At the cross on Calvary, blood flowed from the side of our Savior. The blood that flowed was a different kind of blood than had ever flowed. In fact, the type and foreshadow of Calvary was practiced for hundreds of years as the priests killed the bulls and goats and sprinkled their blood on the mercy seat of the Ark of the Covenant. This was an atonement made for the sins of the people. The word "atone" means "to cover over." However, animal blood could not remit nor cancel sin. Hebrews 10:4 declares, "The blood of bulls and goats cannot take away sin." It could only temporarily cover sin until Jesus came as the only perfect and final sacrifice.

Jesus' blood, and His blood alone, is the only remission for sin. He invites us to come to Him when we are broken, hurt, offended, wounded, or in need. I John 1:9 states, "If we confess our sins, He is faithful and just to forgive us our sins, and to cleanse us from all unrighteousness." Our trust is in His blood. Our faith is in His blood. Our confidence is in His blood. There is no mending of a vessel without blood. There is no way to restore it without blood. Blood is essential to make it whole once again.

We are living in a time when the lives of many people are broken. Some were broken in the process of being used, and some cracked in the heat of the fire. No effective, anointed ministry will ever come from us unless we have been through the fire. The fire produces durability but many times we crack in the fire. Have you ever cracked? Have you have ever had a poor attitude? Have you ever said something you shouldn't have said? Have you ever exploded in anger? You cracked in the fire, in the circumstance or situation, under the pressure. Clearly, we live in a time when pressure and stress are coming against us from nearly every direction.

We are surrounded by people that are very angry inside. If you unintentionally cut someone off in traffic, you'll see what I mean! It's as if anger is boiling inside and waiting for an opportunity to erupt. God will often use circumstances to reveal a crack in our "vessel," but if we run to the blood of Jesus, He will heal it, mend it, make it whole, and He will put us right back into the same fire in which we cracked. We might pray, "God, if You would only put me in a different furnace, I wouldn't crack." But God knows what furnace will make us durable. He knows what people with which to surround us. He knows where to give us employment and which neighborhood in which to have us live. Why? Is God against us? Is He trying to make life difficult for us? No. God is preparing our vessel, and He will repair us by applying the blood when we run to Him. He will forgive us again and again, and we will be put right back into the fire until we become durable.

Cracked in the Fire

In I Peter 4:12, the Apostle Peter spoke of the fiery trial that will try us. He wrote, "Beloved, think it not strange concerning the fiery trial which is to try you, as though some strange thing happened unto you." In the natural sense, Peter was very familiar with fireside experiences. When Jesus was on trial, Peter "cracked" by denying Jesus as he warmed himself by a fire. Peter had said earlier, "I will never deny you, Jesus. You can count on me. I will never do that." But, in the fire, he cracked. Peter said three times, "I don't know Jesus." A few hours after Peter's denial, blood flowed from the wounds of Jesus, and Peter wept bitterly. What was Peter doing? He was repenting. He was saying to the Potter, "Forgive me. I cracked under pressure."

Restored in the Fire

Though Peter cracked in the heat of the fire, Jesus had a plan to restore him in a second fire. John Chapter 21 tells the story of how, after Jesus' death on the cross, the disciples had gone fishing because they had become disillusioned, confused, hurt, wounded, and cracked. When they had not caught any fish, a man on the shore called to them and said, "Children, do you have any meat? Cast your net on the right side." They did so, and soon the net was full of fish! John recognized that the man on the shore was Jesus. He said, "It is the Lord!"

Peter dove into the water and swam to Jesus. On the shore, Jesus was sitting by a fire (John 21:9). It was by *that fire* that Jesus said to Peter, "Do you love Me more than these?" Jesus questioned Peter three times; once for every time he cracked in *the other fire* just days before. Jesus healed and restored Peter in that *second fire*. Jesus had placed Peter right back into the fire, but this time Peter didn't crack. In fact, Peter became so durable that he eventually endured prison, and, according to historical tradition, Peter eventually said, "I am not ashamed of the cross, but I am not worthy to be crucified in the same manner as Jesus. Crucify me upside down." He had become incredibly strong and durable because of the fire. Peter had cracked, but Jesus' blood flowed, and Peter was restored. The Potter wouldn't let go of him. He healed him, but first He put him back into the fire. In the world, failure is often final, but in God, failure is not final! God is a God of restoration and healing.

Isaiah 43:10 declares, "I have chosen you in the furnace of affliction." Many are called, but few are chosen. A lot of people talk about their calling, but it's in the fire where we become durable. Everyone that is ever going to be used by God must go through the fire, but we can be encouraged because we are not alone in the fire. God is with us in the midst of the fire's heat and pressure. In Daniel Chapter 3, when the three Hebrew children (Shadrach, Meschach, and Abednego) were cast into the fiery furnace, they saw a "fourth man" (Jesus) walking with them in the fire. *We have God's presence with us in the fire!*

If You Crack, Run To the Blood

Scripture tells us that we don't *have to* crack. Jude 24-25 declares, "Now unto him that is able to keep you from falling, and to present you faultless before the presence of his glory with exceeding joy, To the only wise God our Saviour, be glory and majesty, dominion and power, both now and ever. Amen." God is able to keep us from cracking, but because of our humanness and the circumstances of this fallen world in which we live, sometimes we do crack. If you have cracked, or if you ever do crack, run to the blood. It is the healing, restoring power of the blood that will take you through. It is the cohesiveness of the blood that matters, not the depth or the length of the crack in your vessel. It is the blood that remits *all* sin. The broken vessel needs the blood!

CHAPTER 10

Vessels of Wrath

Occasionally, for some reason which potters have never been able to understand, a broken vessel will repel, reject, and refuse the blood. These vessels are called vessels of wrath. The potter treats all broken vessels alike. He takes a broken vessel, squeezes the little fasuka, mixes its blood with the clay, and puts the vessel back into the fire. Rarely, but occasionally, a vessel repeatedly rejects the blood of the fasuka and therefore cracks in the fire. After the potter had patiently and repeatedly tried to mend and repair a vessel which repeatedly and consistently rejected the blood, he took it to the wall of the city. Just outside of the city wall, there was a field called Aceldama (Acts 1:19). The potter, knowing this vessel would not take the blood, threw the vessel over the wall, and it usually broke into little pieces.

Lepers came along, took the pieces, and rubbed them across the sores on their body to try to relieve their pain. That field was called the "field of blood," or the "potter's field." Amazingly, according to Acts 1:18-19, this is the field in which Judas' body lay after he committed suicide. Had Judas committed a sin too bad to forgive? No. The only difference between Judas and Peter was that Peter "took the blood" and Judas did not. Although both Peter and Judas both felt badly for what they had done, Peter repented and Judas did not. Peter ran to Jesus' empty tomb in the hope of seeing Him again. Judas took his own life, failing to run to Jesus for restoration.

Vessels of Wrath

Romans 5:9 declares, "Much more then, being now justified by His blood, we shall be saved from wrath through Him." The only difference between the broken vessel and the vessel of wrath is the blood. The blood is what saves us from being a vessel of wrath. God doesn't want anyone to become a vessel of wrath. He doesn't want anyone to be thrown out. Jesus shed His blood and died on the cross so that no one needs to go to a Godless eternity. No one that accepts the blood will ever experience the wrath of God.

The devil will lie to you and tell you otherwise. He will tell you that you have cracked too many times. He will tell you that your situation is hopeless and you are forever useless. He will tell you that God won't take care of your problems. He will tell you that you are so bound you can never be free. The devil is a liar. Run to the blood. No one that runs to the blood will ever become a vessel of wrath.

There is no shortcut to becoming a useful and anointed vessel. We all must go through the fire. There will be trials and tribulations, and through those experiences, God will mold us, shape us, and prepare us. We are not serving God today because we are immune from the fire. We are serving God today because we took the blood and endured the fire. When the potter picked the little fasukas off the bulls and goats and put them in his container, it was effectively a promise that some broken vessel was going to be made whole. When Jesus died on the cross and His blood flowed, it was effectively a promise that if you come to Him, He will not cast you away, but He will heal and restore you.

Run to the Blood

The blood of Jesus is our only hope, our only help, and our only answer. It's the only solution. The issue is not whether we have cracked. The issue is whether we have run to the blood. The issue is not whether we have ever made a mistake. The question is: have you come to Jesus for the cleansing blood? Are you washed in the blood of the Lamb? Are your garments spotless? Are they white as snow? Nobody has to be a vessel of wrath. Nobody—unless you refuse the blood. If you refuse the blood, it doesn't matter how "good" you are, how much you have accomplished, how popular you are, or how wealthy you have become. It is only the blood of Jesus that redeems, justifies, sanctifies, heals, and makes whole.

Every one of us is a vessel in the hands of the Potter. I am certain that every one of us has made mistakes. Romans 3:23 declares that "all have sinned and come short of the glory of God." We have all cracked. We have all been broken. Some of us were broken by someone that was careless and didn't handle us properly. But it is important for us to acknowledge our brokenness and not to minimize it by thinking that it's not as bad as the brokenness of another. Please hear the heart of the Potter saying, "If you simply come back to Me, acknowledge that you have sinned, that you are broken, that you are cracked, that you are wounded, and that you are not whole, I will forgive you and I will wash you in My blood."

That provision is for all people, both those who have never had a personal relationship with Christ, as well as those who have slipped away from Him. Perhaps the pressure of a specific situation or experience in your life, perhaps what someone said to you or did to you, caused you to crack. Perhaps the devil said to you, "You are not worth anything anymore. It's all over. Give up. Quit." It doesn't matter how you became cracked, because Jesus is saying to you that He will make you new again. Restoration is provided for you. If you will come to Jesus, He will forgive you. He will receive you. He will restore you. It's all in the blood of Jesus. Please examine your heart. There isn't any other alternative. It's the blood of Jesus or the wrath of God. It is the blood of Jesus or eternal damnation. Run to the blood!

CHAPTER II

Clean Vessels

Another of the seven vessels that the Bible mentions is the clean vessel. Isaiah 66:20 declares, "And they shall bring all your brethren for an offering unto the Lord out of all nations upon horses, and in chariots, and in litters, and upon mules, and upon swift beasts, to My holy mountain Jerusalem, saith the Lord, as the children of Israel bring an offering in a clean vessel into the house of the Lord."

Clean Vessels

Before we look at the clean vessel and its purpose in more depth, let us quickly review a few things we learned about the vessel of honor, because a clean vessel actually starts out as a vessel of honor. In order to appreciate its condition as a clean vessel, we must be reminded of its original condition and purpose as a vessel of honor.

A vessel of honor was made in a cone-shaped manner with handles attached to each side of the vessel. It generally held about five gallons of water. It was located at the front door of a home and also at the entrance of the temple to provide water for people to wash their feet as they entered a home or the temple. In addition, at the entrance of the temple, people would customarily wash their hands before they prayed. But more importantly than that, the vessel of honor provided fresh water for the thirsty. It was important that every vessel of honor was taken to the well every morning and filled with fresh water which would be made available at the house and the temple for everyone that was thirsty. It was customary that no one would be denied a drink. If you were to walk by a house in that day, the vessel of honor would be sitting outside the door. You would be welcome to drink of this water without asking permission. It was the homeowner's responsibility to make certain that the water was fresh and it had come from the well that very morning.

In Chapter 7 of this book, we interpreted the typology of the vessel of honor, and we applied it to our lives personally. We learned that God wants each of us to be vessels of honor. We need to draw fresh water from Him, the Well of Life, every day, by spending time in prayer, Bible study, and worship. In John Chapter 4, Jesus told the woman at the well that He had water which would satisfy her soul so completely that she would never thirst again. If we are full of the fresh water Jesus offers, then whoever we encounter can receive fresh water from us. We will be able to give them something that is fresh from the Lord, not something that is contaminated or has been sitting around collecting bacteria. I think one of the most wonderful things we have as people of God is to be able to fellowship with other Christians and be refreshed in that fellowship. Have you had the experience of encountering another Christian and after walking away, feeling like you have had a fresh drink of water?

There is nothing that quenches my physical thirst like cold, fresh water. I believe that God wants us to be pourers of fresh water spiritually, so that we may refresh one another. The Apostle Paul wrote in Philemon 1:20, "I do wish, brother, that I may have some benefit from you in the Lord; refresh my heart in Christ." (NIV) Even the great apostle needed to be refreshed spiritually. In order for us to refresh others, we must have fresh water to pour out. God doesn't want us to pour out garbage or stale, stagnant, contaminated water. If we have fresh water, everyone that we encounter can be refreshed simply because they have crossed our path and we have poured upon them.

Vessels In Need of Repair

Over time, constant usage frequently damaged a vessel. Because many people touched it, handled it, and moved it from place to place, the vessel could be affected in any combination of three ways. First, some vessels developed stress cracks. Secondly, some developed a film or scum on the inside which contaminated the water. Thirdly, the lip might have become marred, worn, or chipped from much pouring such that the lip would widen and be unable to pour a direct, straight stream of water from the vessel. If you attempt to use a vessel or a pot with a cracked or broken lip, the contents will spill out uncontrollably when you attempt to pour. In summary, one of three things occasionally happened to vessels of honor: 1) a stress crack, 2) contamination, or 3) a damaged lip.

When a vessel was found to be in that condition, it was taken from its place as the vessel of honor in the front of a house and placed in the rear of the house. It wasn't as visible or as useful anymore, but it wasn't destroyed. It was simply used for a different purpose. It was downgraded to another use. It would be used to carry cereal or grains to the temple at the time of sacrifice or offering, and that is where its name came from. God's commandment was that you couldn't use just any old piece of pottery to carry grains to the temple. You had to use a piece of pottery that was clean, one that was not full of garbage or junk. The potter originally made it to carry fresh water, and though it was still enjoying some degree of usefulness, it was less than what the potter had intended. The vessel was not fulfilling His intended purpose for it.

Intended Purpose

That phrase is very important: *intended purpose*. It refers to the fact that God has an intentional, deliberate, clear, and pre-defined purpose for everything He creates. Isaiah 64 tells us that we are the work of His hand. When God made us, He had a purpose in mind. He did not make us and then try to decide how to use us, or try to determine if we were useful at all. The intention is in the mind of the potter *before* he makes the vessel. He knows what he wants to make and the purpose that it is to serve. That is called *intended purpose*. It is the same in our lives. Regardless of our biological history, we must understand and embrace the fact that God created each of us. It doesn't matter what circumstances surrounded our conception or birth. *All* life comes from God. If you are alive, God created you. He made you. He has an intended purpose in mind for your life. You are the result of premeditated divine design. You were not born by accident or random chance.

In the process of being used and of serving, in the process of ministry, we also, like the vessel of honor, can come into a state of needing repair. We can slip away from functioning in the place of our intended purpose. It doesn't mean that we deliberately turned from God or that we are useless, but we are no longer fulfilling the intended purpose for which the Master Potter had made us.

Six Purpose Robbers

Because of our humanness and the fallen world in which we live, there are many things that threaten to distract us and rob us of our intended purpose. I have identified six things which I believe can be potential "purpose robbers" in our lives. Number one, *we can become weary in well doing*. Number two, *we can become stressed*. Number three, *we can lose vision or sight of our purpose*. There are many things that we have to contend with that are continually interrupting us, demanding our time, and requiring our attention, energy and devotion. These kinds of things can cause us to lose our vision or to lose understanding of our purpose. Number four, *we can experience a diminished sensitivity to other people*. Suddenly we don't care like we used to care. We don't hurt for people like we used to hurt for them. We don't feel for others like we used to feel for others. In fact, the spirit of the world is so self-serving that if we are not careful, we will end up caring only for ourselves. Number five, *we can become mechanical in our service*. That means we continue to do all the right things and go through the motions, but our heart isn't in it anymore. That is tragic. We can become so practiced at the *art* of ministry that we lose the *heart* of ministry. Number six, *our enthusiasm can wane*. Sometimes when people start out serving God, they are so enthusiastic they will run you over if you get in their way. I heard one older Christian say to a younger one, "Don't get so excited. When you get a little more mature, you will settle down." No, that is not maturity. Maturity doesn't diminish your enthusiasm.

As a result of these six things, and others that I am sure we could add to this list, we may not be prepared to pour fresh water as we once did. We say, "Well, I am still hanging in there. I am still part of the work of God. I am still doing this and doing that." When we find ourselves in this situation, <u>our response will determine our future</u>. I don't know of a Christian that I have ever met who hasn't experienced difficult seasons. The issue is not whether we will go through difficult times. The issue is what we do when we find ourselves there. Sometimes, we find ourselves in a difficult season when our vision isn't as clear as it used to be, or we aren't as sensitive to others as we once were, or we are simply stressed out. In such seasons, our intended purpose is no longer being fulfilled. We need to be refreshed or restored.

Back to the Potter's House

On occasion, the clean vessels that were being used to carry grain were collected and taken into the temple. The potter came and took these vessels from the temple to his house, and there he was committed to work on them so that they would be restored to their original intended use. He did whatever needed to be done to restore and repair the vessel. Once it was restored, the vessel would then be upgraded from a clean vessel back to a vessel of honor. It could then once again function fully as a vessel of honor! It could be taken to the well every morning to draw fresh water and be placed at the front of the house or at the entrance of the temple. It was once again a vessel of which the potter was proud, and it was again fulfilling its initially intended purpose.

I believe God's desire is to move all of us into the place where His intended purpose is fulfilled in our lives. When we are not pouring as much fresh water, we are inclined to blame the well. When our vessel is relocated from the front to the back of the house, we blame the person that is running the house. We may complain, "I shouldn't be back here. I should be out there." Perhaps you are at this junction or crossroads in your Christian experience.

When we reach that critical point, we need either refreshing or restoration. There is a difference between the two, and sometimes people get them confused. We must define these two words, _refreshing_ and _restoration_.

Refreshing

Refreshing means "to be replenished; to be renewed in strength and energy." Everyone needs to be refreshed. The most obvious example of that is sleep. We are functional today because we slept last night! We were built to be refreshed not only in body, but also in mind, in soul, and in spirit. The way that

God refreshes us is by giving us rest. Rest refreshes us. In Matthew 11:28-30, Jesus said, "Come unto Me, all you that labor and are heavy laden, and I will give you rest. Take My yoke upon you and learn of Me; for I am meek and lowly in heart: and ye shall find <u>rest</u> unto your souls. For My yoke is easy and My burden is light." Jesus recognized the need for rest during His earthly ministry. On occasion, He said to His disciples, "Come apart and rest for a while."

Restoration

There is also a need for restoration. While refreshing is the replenishing of strength and energy, restoration means "to be brought back to the original condition or position." Restoration is taking a clean vessel and making it a vessel of honor once again. In Joel 2:25, God declared, "I will restore to you the years that the locust hath eaten, the cankerworm, and the caterpillar, and the palmerworm." He was effectively saying, "I am going to bring you back to your original condition." If you need restoration, rest won't suffice. I have heard people say, "I think I need rest," then they drop out of serving in ministry altogether. They do so because they thought they needed refreshing but in reality they needed restoration.

Every time that they would gather these clean vessels at the temple and take them back down to the potter's house, they were effectively saying "It's time for restoration." The clean vessels didn't need to be refreshed. They needed to be <u>restored</u>. God grant us the discernment to know the difference in our own lives.

One of the ways we are restored spiritually is through fasting and prayer. Not many people enjoy fasting. Some people fast in order to lose weight, which of course yields no direct spiritual benefit. I once heard a man say, "I fasted for two weeks, and all I lost was fourteen days." As a pastor, I used to call for times of corporate fasting and prayer in our church, because those are times of restoration. They are not times of refreshing, especially if you are depriving yourself of sleep in order to attend early morning, noontime, and evening prayer gatherings each day. During one "prayer week," after four or five consecutive days of this, I got up extremely early one morning to pray, and as I was walking through the house, bumping into walls, I said, "Jesus, I would only do this for You."

We need restoration. It is vital to our lives and ministries. I have found that if I don't get both rest and restoration, I can't pour pure water, and my sensitivity to others tends to diminish. I therefore can't minister as effectively, and I become unhappy and frustrated. Restoration is vital to walking out our intended purpose. It's not what we want to be that is important. It's what God intended us to be that matters. That is why we will be ineffective, unfulfilled, restless, unhappy, and unsatisfied until we are restored.

When a vessel was taken to the potter's house to be restored, there were four things that the potter did to restore it to its original condition and position.

Restoration Step 1—Empty the Vessel

The first thing that the potter did in the process of restoration was empty the vessel of all of its contents. The process of restoration couldn't truly begin until the vessel was emptied. As we go through life, we collect a lot of things, some of which are good and some of which hinder our usefulness and our intended purpose. Some of the things that we collect must be emptied out as we go to God and honestly say, "I have slipped from what I once was. I need to be restored."

God will begin to empty us, first of all, of *opinions*. We can sometimes be "opinion packrats." When we are facing an issue, if we ask ten people what they think, we might hear at least twenty different opinions. Sometimes we need to lay that all down and empty ourselves of opinions.

We also need to empty ourselves of *unscriptural doctrines*. There are many winds of doctrines, and you can be running to and fro, following every voice, and yet not be sure where you are going. I have seen people in so much confusion that it seems that they don't even know whether to hold the Bible upside down or right side up or whether to begin from the back or the front. Be cautious about formulating your doctrine from books, tapes, and TV shows rather than the Word of God.

We also need to empty ourselves of *disappointments, unrealized expectations, and offenses*. The Apostle Paul wrote to the Christians at Corinth, "I am afraid that just as Eve was deceived by the serpent's cunning, your minds may somehow be led astray from your sincere and pure devotion to Christ." (II Corinthians 11:3 NIV) Sometimes we need to get back to the basics. We must be emptied of all the disappointments, unrealized expectations, offenses, winds of doctrine, and opinions of people. If we can't let go of these things, the restoration process can't continue.

Step Two—Scrubbing the Heart

The second thing that the potter did in the restoration process was use a metal tool to scrape and remove all the film and contamination from inside the vessel. He would hold the vessel tightly, apply some "elbow grease," and scrape off all of that stuff. Remember, the inside of the vessel was called the heart. Our heart collects contamination and garbage along the way, and it needs to be constantly cleansed. "Who shall ascend unto the hill of the Lord? He that has clean hands and a pure heart." (Psalm 24:3-4)

Both James and Peter, in their epistles, wrote, "God resisteth the proud and giveth grace to the humble." (James 4:6, I Peter 5:5) When we become prideful, God has to scrape off that stuff, because He doesn't want to resist us. He wants to give us grace and mercy. He wants to touch us and love us. Therefore, He begins to scrape out our pride by dealing with the deepest motives of our hearts. Hebrews 4:12 declares that "The Word of God is quick and powerful, and sharper than any two-edged sword, piercing even to the dividing asunder of soul and spirit, and of the joints and marrow, and is a discerner of the thoughts and intents of the heart." The intents and motives of our heart can become contaminated and our heart needs to be scraped and scrubbed.

Sometimes our pride creates in us a desire for recognition and honor. Philippians 2:7 states that Jesus "made himself of no reputation." Isn't that interesting? *We spend all of our lives making a reputation, and Jesus spent His life making no reputation.* Jesus humbled Himself, even though His heart was perfect, pure, and uncontaminated. It is vital that we humble ourselves and allow the Lord to scrub our contaminated heart so that we can be restored.

Step Three—Resetting the Lip

In the third step of the restoration process, the potter resets the lip. The lip gets wide and sloppy and the contents come out faster than they should. That is what happens when the mouth gets too wide. Therefore, the potter resets the lip, making it true. He makes it like it was initially shaped when it first came off his wheel. He is concerned about the lip because it was created to pour fresh water. If the lip has become cracked through stress or careless use, it will never be able to serve its intended purpose until it is reset.

The Bible speaks of the evil of the tongue. Proverbs 18:21 declares, "Death and life is in the power of the tongue." Did you know that it takes more muscles to hold the tongue still than it does to move it? It is interesting that God made us that way. Physiologically, you have to work harder to be quiet than to talk. We must ask God to "reset our lip" and then to be careful about the things we say.

X-rated mouths are not reserved for curse words alone. Gossiping is a major problem. It is a dominant way of disrobing a friend. It is so prevalent that we often are unaware that we do it. It is the most common sickness of the tongue, and it is a highly communicable disease. Proverbs 17:9 (RSV) states, "He who repeats a matter alienates a friend." I Corinthians 13:6 in the same translation declares, "Love does not rejoice at wrong, but rejoices in the right." (RSV) The New English Translation states it this way, "Love keeps no score of wrongs; does not gloat over other men's sins, but delights in the truth." (NET) Galatians 6:1 declares what our attitude and conversation should be when a friend or fellow believer falls into sin. "Brethren, if a man be overtaken in a fault, ye which are spiritual, restore such an one in the spirit of meekness, considering yourself lest ye also be tempted." (KJV)

Step Four—Back Into the Fire

In step four of the restoration process, the potter puts the vessel back into the fire. We may pray, "Please God, not the fire. You have emptied me. You have scraped me. You have reset my lip. Please, not the fire! God, if You put me into the fire, I will die." He replies, "Do you promise?" The fire is meant to help us die to our flesh so that we can truly live by the Spirit!

When we experience times like this, we are essentially at a crossroads in our lives. We have the choice to resist restoration and be "downgraded" the rest of our lives. Sadly, I have seen people make the wrong choice and end up cynical, critical, and sarcastic. In their minds, everyone and everything else is always wrong. The result is that they have no fresh water to offer to others.

A scripture that confounded me for years is I Corinthians 9:27 where Paul writes, "I keep under my body lest having preached to others, I myself should become a castaway." I didn't understand it until I learned what the word "castaway" means. It doesn't mean to be cast away into the lake of fire, to be eternally damned, or to go to hell. The word castaway means "put out to pasture." One of the saddest things that can happen in the life of a good racehorse is to be put out to pasture. He has been bred and trained and given the best of care by his owner. He can run like the wind and keep his eyes on the goal, the finish line. He can give himself totally to the race that he is in, and carry whatever load is on his back. He is a horse that can run the course. Then something happens. Perhaps he breaks a leg, loses sight in one or both eyes, or becomes overweight. Perhaps he becomes careless and not as disciplined as he once was. When these things happen, the owner has to shake his head and say, "I must take him out of the race. I won't kill him. He will still live, but I will just put him out to pasture, and he can spend the rest of his days eating grass out in the field."

We should all pray, "Jesus, don't let that happen to me. By Your grace and mercy, I prostrate myself at Your feet. I lie face down at the cross, and I say Jesus, restore me. Restore me again and again." In Jeremiah 18, the prophet said of the potter, "and he made it again." He made it again! *How many times is "again"? It's one more time than the number of times it failed.* A clean vessel was filled with grain and kept in the temple for awhile, but when it was time to collect the clean vessels and take them to the potter's house, the vessel was placed on the potter's table with the intention of restoring it. "Restore me. You know what You intended me to be. You know what You created me to do. Dear Potter, restore me."

Mold Me and Make Me

Lord, mold me and make me, according to Your will, into what I was intended to be. To me, the issue is not whether I am present in the temple, and the issue isn't simply whether I am useful. The issue is whether I fulfill the intended purpose for which I was created. The Apostle Paul wrote in II Timothy 4:7, "I have fought *a* good fight. I have finished *my* course. I have kept *the* faith." *A* fight, *my* course, *the* faith. "And henceforth there is laid up for me a crown of righteousness." Why will Paul get the crown? Because he <u>finished his course</u>. He didn't allow himself to be put out to pasture, but rather he kept on running to the end.

I do not intend to communicate condemnation or guilt. If you are not certain what your course is, don't allow yourself to become frustrated. God never demands of you what you don't know. I encourage you to seek the Lord. Worship Him. Stay at His feet. Prostrate yourself at Calvary. Say, "Lord, You alone know the course which You have charted for my life. Put me on the Potter's wheel." Whenever you come to a place in your life when discouragement comes upon you and unrealized expectations seem to overwhelm you, run back to the Potter's house and say, "Restore me. Restore the years that the locust, the caterpillar, the cankerworm and the palmerworm have eaten. Make me useful once again, oh God."

CHAPTER 12

Chosen Vessels

A chosen vessel was so named because it was the result of the very best work that the potter could produce. It ultimately emerged from the fire without stress cracks or marks of any kind. It was a vessel that had yielded totally and perfectly to the process, and as a result, had come out shaped exactly as he intended. It came out completely durable and whole. The potter was very proud of it, and it was a tangible expression of his talents and skills.

The Potter's Name

The potter turned a chosen vessel upside down and wrote his name on it. In doing so, he was effectively saying, "I don't know where this vessel may go, and I don't know who will use it, but I will never be ashamed of it. I am going to put my name on it, and people will know the name of the potter that created it. They may not know who owns the vessel, but they will know who made it." After the potter wrote his name on a chosen vessel, he would store it in the back room of his pottery shop, usually on a shelf in a dark place. If you were to walk into a pottery shop in that day, there were various kinds of vessels on display in the front of the shop. You could look through all of those vessels, but you wouldn't find a chosen vessel out there on display. However, if you asked the potter, "Do you have a chosen vessel?" you might have seen his eyebrows rise. You might have seen his eyes get wide and a smile come over his face, because he knew that you were shopping for something special. He would go into the back room on the shelf and bring out a chosen vessel. Even today in the pottery shops in Jerusalem, there are special vessels with the potter's name on them that are hidden in the back. They are not necessarily in open view. They are not available for everyone to see or touch. These are vessels that are very special to the potter. They are chosen vessels.

David the Chosen Vessel

I Samuel 16:1-13 tells the story of the anointing of David. In that passage of Scripture, the word "chosen" is used repeatedly. God told Samuel, "Go down to Bethlehem, to the household of Jesse. I have chosen one of Jesse's sons to sit on the throne. You are to anoint him. He is going to live for My glory." Samuel went there and said to Jesse, "I need to see your sons." Jesse brought his eldest seven sons and lined them all up. He was so proud of the first one, Eliab, and possibly thought, "He must be the one." Samuel said, "No. He is not the one the Lord has chosen." Jesse may have thought, "Well, then maybe it's the next one, Abinadab. He certainly is a good-looking guy." "No," Samuel said, "the Lord hasn't chosen this one." Jesse may have suggested next, "Well, then maybe it's Shammah." Samuel said, "No. It's not Shammah."

Samuel considered all seven of the young men, but chose none of them. Then he said to Jesse, "Do you have any more sons?" "Oh, yes," Jesse said, "I've got one more, but he is in the 'back room.' He is out in the fields, tending the sheep." You see, God had already been working in that young boy's life. He had been molding his heart. He had been shaping him and preparing him. Young David had been out there among the sheep singing songs unto the Lord, and he had already developed an intimate relationship with God. As soon as Jesse called him in from the field, Samuel said, "That is him. That is the one the Lord has chosen." He said, "Man looks at the outward appearance, but the Lord looks at the heart." (I Samuel 16:7 NIV) God looks at something beyond what we see when He chooses His vessels.

Paul the Chosen Vessel

There is another person in the Bible that was a chosen vessel. He wrote a large portion of the New Testament. His name was Saul of Tarsus, but after the Lord changed his heart and called him into ministry, He changed his name to Paul and wrote His name on him. Although we can't verify Paul's physical appearance from Scriptural evidence, historians and theologians believe that Paul was not a particularly attractive man. If their descriptions are accurate, he was a short, bald, very bowlegged man. He was not the kind of man that was physically appealing, but God saw something in him that He could greatly use for His purposes.

Acts Chapter 9 tells the story of Saul's dramatic conversion experience. Acts 9:10-19 states, "There was a certain disciple at Damascus named Ananias; and to him said the Lord in a vision, 'Ananias.' And he said, 'Behold, I am here, Lord.' And the Lord said unto him, 'Arise and go into the street which is called Straight, and inquire in the house of Judas for one called Saul, of Tarsus; for, behold, he prayeth, and hath seen in a vision a man named Ananias coming in, and putting his hand on him, that he might receive his sight.' Then Ananias answered, 'Lord, I have heard by many of this man how much evil he hath done to the saints at Jerusalem, and here he hath authority from the chief priest to bind all that call on Thy name.' But the Lord said unto him, 'Go thy way, for he is a <u>chosen vessel</u> unto Me to <u>bear My name</u> before the Gentiles and kings and the children of Israel, for I must show him how great things he must suffer for My name's sake.' And Ananias went his way and entered into the house, and putting his hands on him said, 'Brother Saul, the Lord, even Jesus that appeared unto thee in the way as thou camest hath sent me that thou mightest receive thy sight and be filled with the Holy Ghost.' And immediately there fell from his eyes as it had been scales, and he received sight forthwith, and arose and was baptized. And when he had received meat, he was strengthened. And then was Saul certain days with the disciples which were at Damascus. And straightway he preached Christ in the synagogues, that He <Jesus Christ> is the Son of God."

Saul had been on a mission of persecuting the church, beating Christians and imprisoning them for preaching the message that he himself, ironically, would eventually preach. As Saul was on his way to Damascus, he was suddenly interrupted by a sovereign visitation of God. As he lay in the dust, he looked up and said, "Who art Thou, Lord?" That was the beginning of a mighty work of God preparing a vessel for His glory. Saul immediately was struck blind. He was led to a particular house on a street called Straight in Damascus, to the home of a tanner named Judas, where he was given lodging. For three days and three nights, all he knew was darkness, very much like Jonah while he was in the belly of the great fish.

Ananias Obeys

At the end of three days, God spoke to one of His followers, Ananias. Ananias was not an apostle, but he was well known, and he was a man who obviously was accustomed to going to the spiritual well every morning. Ananias was apparently a vessel of honor. One day, Ananias was "at the well," talking to the Lord. The Lord said to him, "I want you, my vessel of honor, to go to Judas' house on Straight Street, and pour fresh water on a man called Saul. Lay hands on him, and he will receive his sight, and he will be filled with the Holy Ghost. He is a vessel that I have *chosen*."

Ananias struggled with God's instructions. Perhaps he thought that God didn't have the most current information. He said, "Lord, are You sure about all of these things? This guy Saul is not a friend of Christians. He has been after us and wants to kill us." God said, "Just go ahead and pour water, and let Me take care of the rest." Ananias went in obedience to God's word. I like the way that Ananias greeted Saul. He called Saul "brother." He didn't call him "enemy;" he called him "brother." Whether Saul had been saved in his Damascus Road encounter with Jesus or whether he was about to get saved when Ananias' hands were laid on him, we are not certain. When Ananias called Saul "brother," he was either acknowledging what God had done, or he was prophesying what God was about to do. In any event, he was open to Saul and he was not pre-judging him. It is important to receive and accept every person whom God sends into our life, as Ananias did. As he laid his hands on Saul, God began to work in Saul and make him into a chosen vessel.

Carrying His Name

God turned Saul upside down and wrote His name on him. He effectively said, "I want you to preach Jesus Christ. My name is on you from now on. Wherever you go, people are going to wonder where you are coming from. They are going to wonder how you changed so completely. They are going to see My name, Jesus Christ, on you." Paul, as Saul came to be called, later wrote to the church at Philippi and recounted how something incredible took place deep in his heart. He effectively wrote in Philippians 3:4-8, "All of the things that I counted gain; all of the accomplishments, all of the credits that I had been accumulating in my life, suddenly became worthless. They became meaningless and as dung. They are nothing in comparison to winning Christ and having His name on me."

The things that became worthless by comparison were things that Paul said he could boast about in the flesh. Look again at Philippians 3:4-8. Paul said, "I was circumcised the eighth day." He effectively said, "It doesn't mean a thing. Of the stock of Israel, it doesn't mean a thing." He was from the "tribe of Benjamin." Not everyone could say that, but it was no longer important to him! He was "a Hebrew of the Hebrews. It doesn't mean a thing. Concerning the law, I was a Pharisee." Pharisee—*yeccch*! He said two other things. "Concerning zeal, I was persecuting the church." Then the last thing he said, "There is one more thing that God emptied out of me, and it's also part of the dung." He said, "Concerning the righteousness that is in the law, I was blameless." Who else can say that? Nobody that I know of! But Paul now considered his own righteousness to be worthless. He effectively said, "Jesus turned me upside down, emptied me, and wrote His name on me. That means more to me than anything else. I am going to be a chosen vessel to carry His name." Sometimes we want to use the name of Jesus like a credit card that we pull out of our pocket and slap down to get our way or do our own thing. That is not its purpose. God said, "When people take a look at you, even when you are upside down, they are going to see My name."

A Worldwide Ministry

God spoke through Ananias and mentioned three things that were going to happen to Paul, His chosen vessel. First, Paul would carry His name, as we discussed above.

Secondly, Acts 9:16 declares, "You are going to bear it before the Gentiles, the kings, and the children of Israel." He effectively said to Paul, "I am going to make you an apostle to the Gentiles. You are a chosen vessel, and I am going to give you a worldwide ministry." Paul preached for thirty years after his conversion and he had a team of five people that worked with him. One was Timothy, who was half Greek and half Hebrew. Another was Luke the physician, who was Greek. Paul also had two Macedonians and one Asiatic on his ministry team. The composition of Paul's ministry team was worldwide in nature, and God sent him out to the known world. In Romans 1:14, Paul said, "I am a debtor to the Greeks and the Barbarians and the wise and the unwise." He was effectively saying, "I am indebted to the world. God has put His name on me, He has called me, and He has sent me outside of my own comfortable surroundings. I am a good Jew. I have attained and accomplished much, and others look up to me. But God took me, and He sent me to regions unknown, outside of my comfort zone."

The third thing God said to Ananias about this chosen vessel is found in Acts 9:16. God told Paul, "I am going to show you how great things you must suffer for My namesake." He said, "In order to carry My name, in order to bear My name to whomever I will send you, there is a cost. There is a price. And I am going to show it to you, Paul. It's called suffering."

Suffering

Most people don't like to talk about suffering. I don't like to talk about suffering either, but it's in the Bible. When the word "suffering" is used, it is not referring to physical illnesses or ailments. Suffering is defined two ways in the New Testament. First of all, it means "mistreatment by people." People are going to mistreat you. The second definition of it is "harassed by the enemy." God was effectively telling Paul, "The enemy is going to dedicate himself to giving you a difficult time. This is because you are carrying My name, Paul. Don't take it personally. It's not the shape of your vessel, but rather the name of the potter, that's causing the stir. The name on the bottom of the vessel, Jesus Christ, is the name on which you stand."

Paul later wrote about his experiences as a chosen vessel who had learned how to suffer. He wrote in II Corinthians 11:20-28, "You suffer if a man bring you into bondage, if a man devour you, if a man take of you, if a man exalt himself, if a man smite you on the face. I speak as concerning reproach as though we had been weak. Howbeit whereinsoever any is bold, I speak foolishly. I am bold also. Are they Hebrews? So am I. Are they Israelites? So am I. Are they the seed of Abraham? So am I. Are they ministers of Christ? I speak as a fool. I am more. In labors more abundant, in stripes above measure, in prisons more frequent, in deaths often. Of the Jews five times I received thirty-nine stripes. Thrice I was beaten with rods. Once I was stoned. Thrice I suffered shipwreck. A night and a day I have been in the deep. In journeyings often, in perils of waters, in perils of robbers, in perils by mine own countrymen, in perils by the heathen, in perils in the city, in perils in the wilderness, in perils in the sea, in perils among false brethren, in weariness and painfulness, in watchings often, in hunger and thirst, in fastings often, in cold and nakedness. Beside those things that are without, that which cometh upon me daily, the care of all the churches."

Obedience

Obviously, Paul suffered greatly as a chosen vessel bearing the name of the Lord Jesus Christ. When I read that, I feel ashamed, because we tend to complain about the silliest little things. Have you have been beaten five times with thirty-nine stripes, three times with a rod, or shipwrecked three times for the cause of Christ? Has your life ever been in danger because of sharing your faith? Paul's was, many times. Paul's worldwide ministry cost him dearly. Jesus, who preceded Paul by a few years, had talked a little bit about that Himself. He told His disciples that a servant is not greater than his lord, and Hebrews 5:8 declares that Jesus "learned obedience by the things which He suffered." The same Greek word translated "suffered" in Hebrews 5:8 was used when Ananias prophesied over Paul. There was power and authority and anointing without measure in the life of Jesus because of His obedience to the Father, which came about as a result of the suffering that He experienced. Some things came to Jesus by gift, and other things came by learning. Obedience is not a gift. *Obedience is a product of learning.* Sometimes the hardest thing for our human nature to do is to obey. Jesus was obedient, and He paid a steep price. He was blasphemed, denied, betrayed, beaten, falsely accused, and finally crucified.

Paying the Price

In 67 A.D., the Apostle Paul, a *chosen vessel*, was beheaded for the Gospel of Christ according to historical tradition. Jesus had said, "Many are called, but few are chosen." (Matthew 22:14) The same Greek word translated "chosen" is used in that statement by Jesus, and also in Acts 9:15, where God calls Paul His chosen vessel. Jesus turned to His disciples one day before He went away and said, "You have not chosen me, but I have chosen you, and ordained you that you should go and bring forth fruit and that your fruit should remain." (John 15:16) Once again, it's the same Greek word translated "chosen." The disciples did as Jesus said, and they experienced mistreatment from men and harassment from the enemy. The enemy hates and fears a chosen vessel of the Lord. That is why we need to pray for one another.

Prayer is vitally important. A chosen vessel automatically becomes a target of the enemy.

In Philippians 3, Paul effectively wrote, "I call all of these accomplishments and accolades 'dung' because there are three things I want which are more important than anything else: I want to know Him, I want to know the power of His resurrection, and I want to know the fellowship of His sufferings."

First, Paul declared, "I want to know Him." That word "know" in the Greek means "have intimate fellowship and communion; to have a relationship." This is not just referring to having intellectual knowledge *about* someone. Paul wrote, "I want to know *Him*."

Secondly, Paul declared, "I want to know the power"—the *dunamis*, explosive miraculous power—"of His resurrection." This is where we tend to put a period, but the Holy Spirit put a conjunction—the word "and" which ties these thoughts together. In fact, all three of these thoughts are tied together. Paul wrote in Philippians 3:10 of his desire that "I might know him *and* the power of His resurrection *and* the fellowship of His sufferings, being made conformable unto his death, if by any means I might attain unto the resurrection of the dead." In the original Greek text, the word "first" precedes the word resurrection, in effect making it say "that I might attain unto the *first* resurrection of the dead." The first resurrection of the dead refers to salvation in Christ.

Thirdly, Paul understood that to fulfill his calling as a chosen vessel and bring the power of the resurrection to the gentile world, there would be a cost. He did not shrink from the cost. He said, "I will pay the price. I want the power of the resurrection so much that I will embrace the fellowship of His sufferings."

The anointing that God wants to grant us, both as individuals and as a church, will not come without a cost. We can get excited as we clap and jump and shout about power, but we don't have anywhere near the power we need. We must have a resolve and a determination in our hearts. We must make a quality decision to persevere in our walk with Jesus no matter what happens—no matter what people say, whatever we have to deal with, or whatever the enemy tries to throw at us. Everything that Paul had accomplished in his own power would disappear someday, but the call of Jesus on his life had eternal significance and reward. So also with us.

CHAPTER 13

Vessels of Mercy

The Apostle Paul, God's chosen vessel, wrote about "vessels of mercy" in his letter to the church at Rome. Romans 9:23 states, "That He," speaking of Jesus, "might make known the riches of His glory on vessels of mercy, which He had afore prepared unto glory." Vessels of mercy, like chosen vessels, were vessels of honor, but their use was different. Again, the vessel of honor sat near the door of the house and just inside the door of the temple. It contained five gallons of fresh water which was drawn from the well every morning. When someone would go to another's house or the temple, they could receive of this water. The vessel of honor is a picture of God's heart, love, and compassion, and there is even a greater revelation of Him through "vessels of mercy."

Vessels of Mercy

Vessels of mercy were filled daily with fresh water at the well, like the vessel of honor, but were placed instead in a <u>public place</u>, such as in the middle of a town square, on a windowsill, or on a fence wall. Vessels of mercy existed to serve. No one knew to whom a vessel of mercy belonged, because it did not carry its owner's name. The only name on it was the name of the potter who made it. Any stranger or wanderer that walked through town who was tired and weary and in need of refreshment could be ministered to by this vessel. It was placed there in the morning without any knowledge of who it was going to serve. Its presence said in effect, "I am available to you. I am free. I care about you. I will refresh you. I will nourish you. I will bless you, if you just drink from me." There is always a provision in the plan of God for a drink of water for the sick, the hurting, the needy, the tired, the lonely, and the lost.

Please see the heart of God as shown through this vessel. The vessel was meant to minister to whoever would come along. You could say that this represents the worldwide vision of God—to reach out beyond our comfort zone. If any church is going to move in obedience to the purpose of God, it must have a worldwide vision, a vision that is not limited to its own four walls. We must understand that God's provision is for the marketplace, wherever we may be. You may think that you are working in the midst of the biggest group of sinners you have ever encountered. You might even pray, "God, if You would only get me out of here, I could live a victorious life. Let me work with a group of Christians." Perhaps He has placed you right where you are to be His vessel of mercy. Your mission is not to find another location, but rather to get filled with fresh water every day and become a vessel of mercy to the thirsty people around you.

You might say, "But I feel so used." So did the vessel of mercy. Someone would walk by, pick it up, take a drink, set it down, and then keep on going. Jesus said if we give a cup of cold water to one that is thirsty, our reward will be certain (Matthew 10:42, Mark 9:41). Sometimes we view ministry as something that requires years of training or certain outstanding abilities, but Jesus wants us simply to begin to blossom where we are planted and begin to pour water where He has placed us. You may say, "Lord, I don't want to sit on a windowsill. I want to be in the temple." If you can't function on the windowsill or the fence wall, forget about the temple. The vessel of mercy is a very special vessel, because it gets handled continually by many people with dirty hands and dirty lips. God said, "This is what your town needs. This is what your world needs. This is what your workplace needs. This is what your school needs. That is why I put you where you are. Your mission is to get filled with fresh water every morning and be ready to pour it out."

Blessed are the Merciful

In I Corinthians 3:6, Paul (formerly Saul) spoke of how one sows and another waters, but God gives the increase. Sometimes we are so preoccupied with seeing the increase that we think nothing of worth has been accomplished unless we see immediate results. Can we not be satisfied to simply be one who waters? Someone is going to become weak and they are not going to make it along the road of life unless there is a vessel of mercy sitting there, waiting to pour into them. Jesus said, "Blessed are the merciful, for they shall obtain mercy." (Matthew 5:7) We all need mercy. Give it out. Stop the harshness and the criticism. Give mercy liberally. You might think, "But I am afraid if I don't straighten things out, someone is going to mess up the kingdom." Jesus can run the kingdom. He ran it before we got here and He will be running it after we are gone. I have had people come to me complaining, "There are no open doors. Nobody invites me. The Bible instructs us to be prepared to give an answer for the hope that is within you when you are asked, and nobody is asking me for anything." Well, I believe if we are filled with cool, fresh water, thirsty people are going to line up for a drink from us.

When I was a boy in school, we would all run to get in line at the drinking fountain at recess or break time, because the fountain had something we wanted and needed. We would try to make friends with the kids in the front of the line, so that we could "take cuts," essentially jumping ahead in the line to the front. It was all about a group of children that were thirsty and needed a cool drink. Likewise, the world is thirsty and even dying of thirst. Many people are trying to supply their own water, but it doesn't last. They are like the woman at the well (John 4), who effectively said, "I have had six husbands, and now I have another man, and I am just trying to be fulfilled." The world needs Jesus, who said to that woman, "When you drink of Me, you will never thirst again. I will satisfy."

From "Give Me" to "Make Me"

There is a cost to being a chosen vessel or a vessel of mercy. I can summarize it with the term "self-denial." I do not live for myself. I do not live to please myself. I do not live to fulfill my agenda. I have been made by the hand of the Potter. He has put His name on me, and, therefore, I am not a debtor to self. Like Paul, I am a debtor to the Greeks and the Barbarians and the wise and the unwise. (Romans 1:14) I am a debtor to those for whom Jesus died.

Don't spend your life selfishly putting things into your own vessel. The prodigal son did that, and he ended up lonely, destitute, heartbroken, and separated from his home and his father. In his youth, he had a "give me" mentality. He demanded that his father <u>give</u> him his inheritance early, and he subsequently squandered it trying to please his flesh. Ultimately, he recognized that being a servant in his father's house was better than living in frustration out in the world. He prepared a speech in which he was going to ask his father to <u>make</u> him one of his servants. *The prodigal son had gone from a "give me" to a "make me" mentality.* His father never gave him the chance to deliver his entire speech, because the father embraced him and warmly received him back home with forgiveness and great joy, not just as a servant, but as his son.

I want God to make me into all that He intended for me to be and to place me wherever He chooses. Somehow, we must look beyond the sacrifices we make today and look forward to the days of harvest and the reward which will follow. We need to pray, "Make me a blessing, Lord. Make me a blessing to someone today."

CHAPTER 14

The Potter and You

I trust you know and understand that you are not alive by accident or random occurrence, but rather you are a vessel designed by a loving master Potter for a divine purpose. God is the Potter, and you are the clay. You are indeed a special vessel, the work of the Potter's hands. Many of the things that you have experienced in life are simply part of the process in which He is "making" and forming you into the very person, the "vessel," that He has always intended for you to be. Don't resist the process, but rather embrace it, though it is sometimes difficult. If you do, your life will be an adventure and a journey that will lead you toward God's intended purpose for your life.

You can know the Potter personally. He wants to have a personal relationship with you. It is only in knowing the Potter that you can truly discover who you were intended to be, and how you can live out His intended purpose, which results in a fulfilling, productive life. The Potter is active and involved in your life, watching over you, guiding you gently but firmly back to the center of His will, and restoring you when you've been broken throughout the course of life. The Potter will not discard you nor turn His back on you, even when you have failed Him or forsaken Him. Instead, He will wrap His strong hands around you, hold you, mend you, and form you. You can trust the Potter. You can trust Him with your life, and I encourage you to do that very thing. Yield your life to Him right now.

Give Him control and let Him use you to fulfill your intended purpose.

You Are Special

You are not just "any old vessel." You are a unique, one-of-a-kind vessel. You are very special and precious to the Potter. The Potter loves you so much that He would die for you. In fact, He did exactly that, over 2000 years ago. He couldn't stand the thought of seeing you broken and separated from Him for eternity, so He left the perfection of heaven and came to earth and took on the form of a human vessel Himself. Jesus Christ was fully God and yet fully man. He was divinity wrapped in humanity. He came to earth and lived a perfect life, satisfying the Father's requirement of a perfect sinless sacrifice as He died on the cross. On the cross, Jesus "took on" your sins and paid the price for your sins. Three days later, He rose from the dead to show that He has power over sin and death, and He can give you new life.

It doesn't matter what you've done or how "bad" you've been. It doesn't matter if you have been a "vessel of dishonor." We have all sinned and have fallen short of the glory of God. Because of what Jesus did on the cross, you can be totally and completely forgiven of your sins, washed white as snow, and you can spend eternity with Him in heaven. To receive this free gift of salvation, which you can never earn through good works, you must believe that Jesus is God's Son and the only Savior, and you must repent. The word "repent" means to make a conscious decision to turn away from your sins and make a commitment to follow Jesus. The Potter isn't looking for vessels who will just give Him "lip service." He is looking for vessels who will give Him their heart.

THE WORK OF THE POTTER'S HANDS

A Prayer from the Heart, and a New Life

The exact words aren't important, but the sincerity of your heart is. This is an intimate moment between the Potter and you. Whisper a prayer to Him right now along these lines: "Jesus, I come to You just as I am. I acknowledge that I am a sinner, and I have fallen short in so many ways. But I believe that You lovingly created me, You love me, You died on the cross for me as my Savior, and You rose from the dead to give me new life. I repent of my sins. Please forgive me and wash me clean. Give me a new start in life, fix my cracked and broken areas, and help me to please You and fulfill Your intended purpose for me here on the earth. Thank You for loving me, Jesus, and for giving me the incredible gift of eternal life and the privilege of spending eternity in heaven with You, where there will be no more tears, no more pain, no more brokenness, and no more death. I love you Jesus, and I surrender my life to You as my Lord. Thank You for saving my soul and filling me with Your Holy Spirit. Draw me close to You and help me to grow closer to You each and every day. Amen."

If you prayed that prayer in the sincerity of your heart, you are a new person in Christ! You are born again. Life here on earth will never be perfect, but now that you have placed your life in the hands of the Potter, He will be right by your side as you walk in a new, wonderful, personal relationship with Him. Make time to go to the well every day, spending time in prayer, Bible study, worship, and meditation. Get involved with a Bible-believing church and serve there with all your heart. I believe that as you do these things, God will fill your vessel with fresh life-giving water and you will pour it out to others. You can discover and fulfill the Potter's intended purpose for your life. You are the work of the Potter's hands!

There is a poem called "The Potter's Vessel" by Beulah V. Cornwall that carries a beautiful message, and I think it is fitting that I close this book with these touching and powerful words.

The Potter's Vessel

The Master was searching for a vessel to use.
On a shelf there were many, Which one would he choose?
"Pick me," cried the gold one. "I'm shiny and bright;
I'm of great value and I do things just right.
My beauty and my luster will outshine the rest,
And for someone like you, Master, I would be best."

But the Master passed on with no word at all.
He came to a silver urn. It was narrow and tall.
"I'll serve you, dear Master, and I'll pour your wine,
And I'll be at your table whenever you dine.
My lines are so graceful and my carvings so true,
And my silver would always complement you."

Unheeding, the Master passed on to the brass.
It was wide mouthed and shallow and polished like glass.
"Here, here," cried the vessel. "I know I will do.
Place me on your table for all men to view."

"Look at me," cried the goblet of crystal so clear.
"My transparency shows my contents are dear.
Though fragile am I, I'll serve you with pride,
And I'm sure I'd be happy in your house to abide."

THE WORK OF THE POTTER'S HANDS

But the Master came next to a vessel of wood.
Polished and carved, it solidly stood.
"Use me, dear Master," the wooden bowl said,
"But I'd rather you use me for fruit; please, no bread."

Then the Master looked down and saw a vessel of clay.
Empty, broken, it helplessly lay.
No hope had that vessel that the Master might choose,
To cleanse and make whole, to fill or to use.

"Ah, this is the vessel I've been hoping to find.
I'll mend it, and I'll use it, and I'll make it all mine.
I need not a vessel with pride in itself,
Nor the one so narrow who sits on the shelf,
Nor the one who is big mouthed and shallow and loud,
Not the one who displays its contents so proud,
Not the one who thinks he can do all things just right,
But rather this plain earthen vessel filled with My power and might."

Then gently he lifted the vessel of clay.
He mended and cleansed it and filled it that day.
He spoke to it kindly, "There's work you must do.
You pour out to others, and I'll pour into you."

More Inspirational Books from Pastor Leonard Gardner

Eight Principles of Abundant Living

In this inspiring and thought provoking book, Pastor Gardner examines each recorded miracle in the Book of John to uncover spiritual principles of abundant living which can lead you into a lifestyle of deep satisfaction, joy, fulfillment, and true happiness.

The Unfeigned Love of God

This powerful and heart-touching book, derived from a series of sermons by Pastor Gardner, will help you understand, accept, and embrace the incredible love which God seeks to lavish on you.

Walking Through the High and Hard Places

The key to a fulfilling life is learning to "walk through" whatever situation or circumstance you encounter. The spiritual principles you learn in *Walking Through the High and Hard Places* will give you the strength to handle any circumstance in life!

www.liberatingword.org

Coming Soon from Pastor Leonard Gardner

- The Blood of the Lamb
- Chosen to Follow Jesus
- The Blood Covenant
- Principles of Prayer

To…
…receive Pastor Gardner's free monthly newsletter;
…schedule him for a ministry meeting at your church;
…or order his books or other resources,

Contact him at:

Liberating Word Ministries
Pastor Leonard Gardner
PO Box 380291
Clinton Township, MI 48038
Phone: (586) 216-3668
Fax: (586) 416-4658
lgardner@liberatingword.org

Made in the USA
San Bernardino, CA
09 February 2015